The Eternal Plan of God

Dispensations - Covenant Promises - Salvation

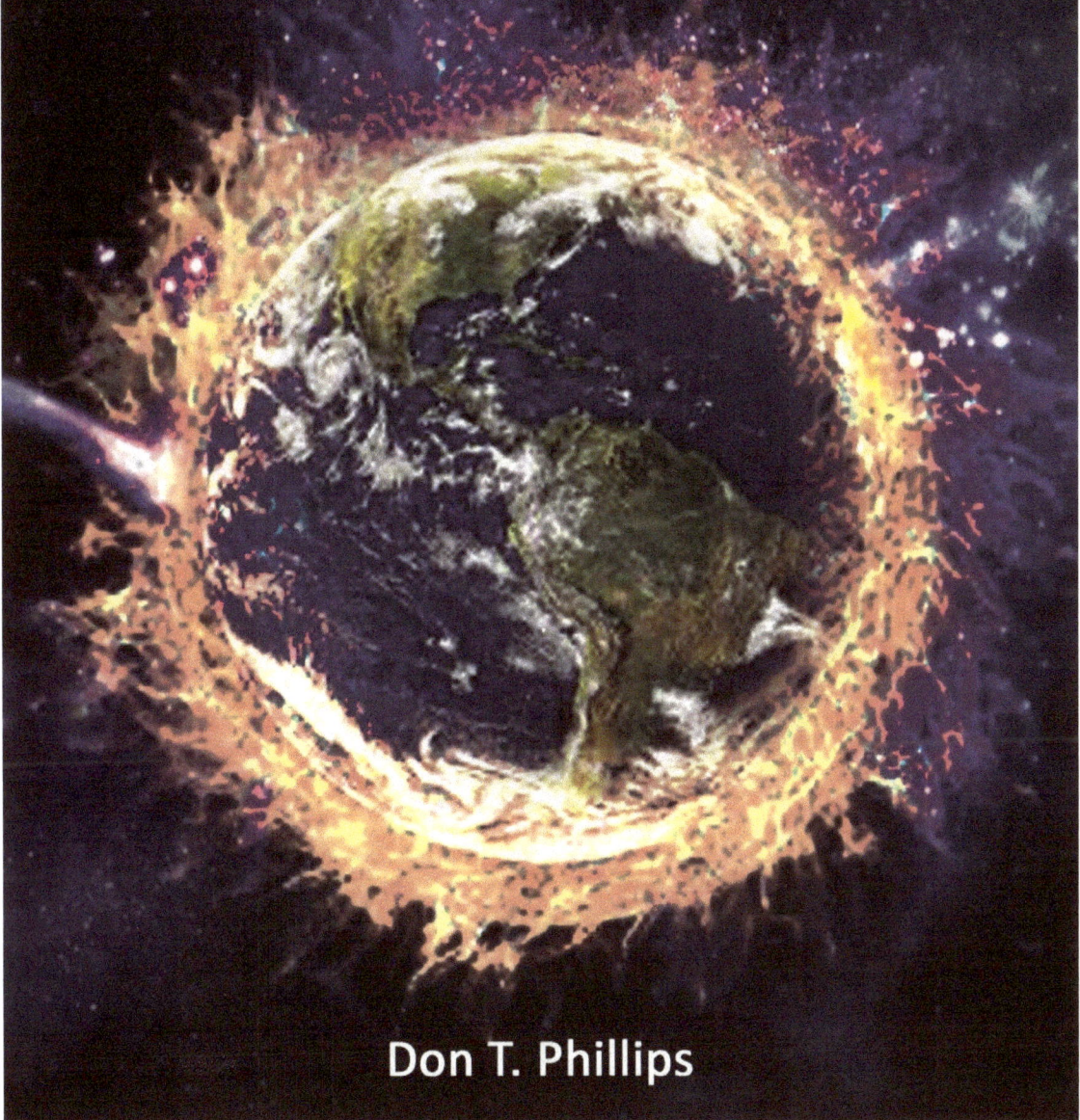

Don T. Phillips

"The Eternal Plan of God: Dispensations - Covenant Promises – Salvation," by Don T. Phillips. ISBN 978-1-62137-871-6 (casebound).

Published 2016 by Virtualbookworm.com Publishing Inc., P.O. Box 9949, College Station, TX 77845, US.

The Eternal Plan of God

Dispensations-Covenants-Salvation

By

Dr. Don T. Phillips

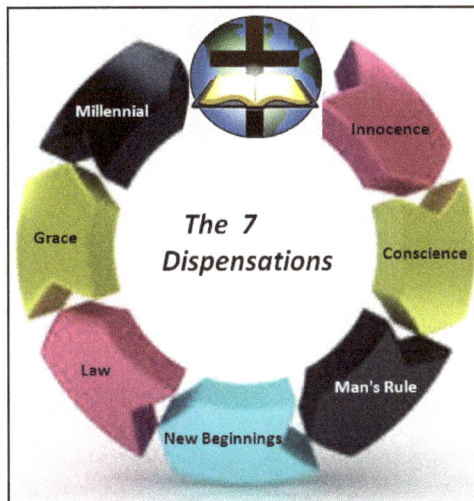

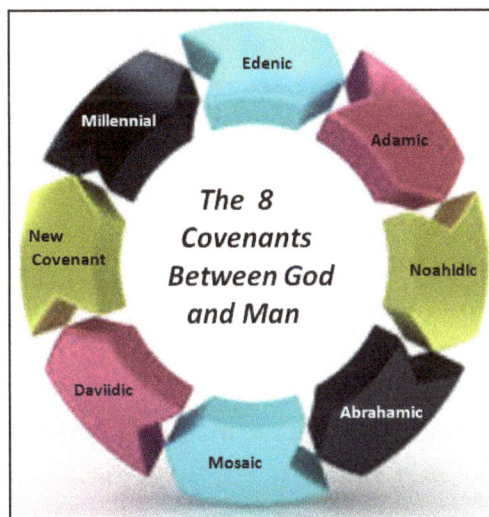

PREFACE

The average Western World Christian spends little time studying and trying to understand the Old Testament and how it fits into the framework and spiritual truths of the New Testament. This is very unfortunate, because God has chosen to show us things in the Old Testament which reinforces and underscores many of the teachings in the New Testament. The New Testament gospels and epistles quote the Old Testament a total of 855 times.

New Testament Book	Old Testament Quotations
The Gospel of Matthew	96
The Gospel of Matthew	34
The Gospel of Matthew	58
The Gospel of Matthew	40
The Book of Acts	57
Romans	74
I Corinthians	41
II Corinthians	13
Galatians	16
Ephesians	11
Philippians	3
Colossians	3
I Thessalonians	2
II Thessalonians	2
I Timothy	6
II Timothy	2
Hebrews	86
James	16
I Peter	20
II Peter	10
I John	6
Revelation	249

https://www.blueletterbible.org/study/pnt/pnt08.cfm

Jesus Christ the Messiah quoted 49 different Old Testament verses (not including the repeats of the same verses throughout the different books) from 27 books of the Old Testament. The Old Testament was and still is the Word of God which was sent to us by divine revelation. The entire counsel of scripture is intended to give us wisdom and strengthen our faith.

We are saved by *faith,* and faith comes by *hearing;* and hearing by the *word of God.*

> **So then faith cometh by hearing, and hearing by the word of God.**
> Romans 10:17

God has revealed Jesus Christ by *Progressive Revelation* that starts in the Book of Genesis and continues all the way through the Book of Revelation. It is important that we rightly *divide the word of God* as it has been given to us by prophets chosen by God to reveal His divine nature. The following diagram was first constructed by Clarence Larkin almost 150 years ago. Larkin divided the scope of human history into 7 different periods of time.

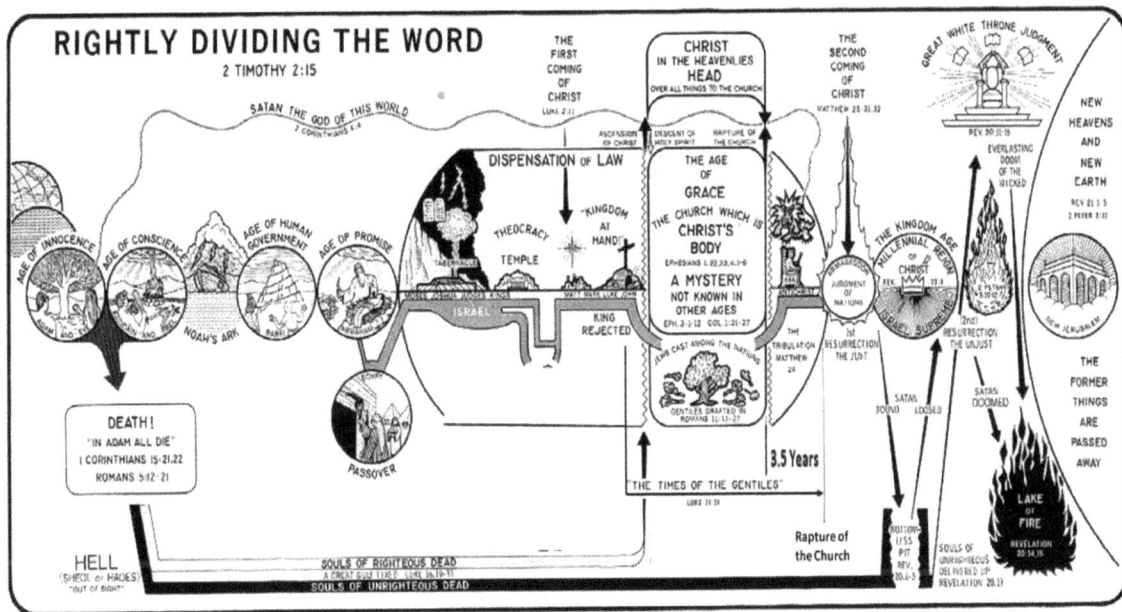

Clarence Larkin (1850-1924)

In this book we will also divide the entire Biblical Record into seven different, mutually exclusive, epochs of time which will be called *dispensations.* A Biblical Dispensation is a fixed period of time in which God relates to man in a distinct and preordained manner.

Just as God has dealt with His creation, and continues to deal with mankind, there is another way to characterize the divine nature of YAWH other than the seven different dispositions of recorded time. This is by a *Covenant Relationships* that

God has established with man. In this book we will define and scripturally characterize eight different covenants that God has "cut" or made with mankind. Each covenant that God has made with man promises to bless or punish mankind based upon whether a covenant (promise) is *conditional* or *unconditional*. If God makes an unconditional covenant promise, He will honor that promise regardless of what man may or may not do. If God and man engage in conditional promises, God is not obligated to fulfill His promises to man if they violate the conditions of the covenant. We will study each of eight major covenants established between God and man to determine which were made null and void by man, and which are still in effect today.

As God dealt with mankind through recorded time, He established several *signs* of His omnipotent and omnipresent nature. We will define and study 11 distinct signs; eight have already been put into place and three are still future. The seven different *Dispensations*, the eight different *covenants*, and the eleven distinct *signs,* taken both individually and collectively, can be understood as biblical truths that if carefully studied relate to and define the *Eternal Plan of God*. The Eternal Plan of God has always been only one thing; to bring mankind into a personal relationship with God by accepting His Son Jesus Christ as the Savior of the World, and be granted salvation and eternal life by *faith*. By *faith*, one believes that Jesus Christ is the only begotten Son of God who died for the sins of the world and was resurrected from the dead. He was the *firstfruit* of many sons and daughters who would be saved by His sacrificial death on the cross of Calvary.

It is hoped that this study will edify the body of Christ, clearly establish the plan of salvation, and bring someone into an intimate relationship with Jesus Christ. For both born-again Christians and all those who seek a better understanding of the Holy Scriptures, it is hoped that this book will fulfill expectations. May God bless us by studying His Holy Word.

Dr. Don T. Phillips
August 1, 2016
College Station, Texas

Acknowledgements

This book is dedicated to those biblical scholars who have pioneered the study of dispensations and covenants and how they have identified and characterized the events which have occurred throughout biblical recorded history. There are many individuals who have unified and characterized these important concepts. There are several individuals that have been particularly influential to me as this book was compiled.

Dr. Charles Ryrie

Dr. Clarence Larkin

Dr. John G. Hall

Dr. J. Dwight Pentecost

Dr. John F. Walvoord

Shonnie Scott

Dr. Arnold Fruchtenbaum

In the course of compiling this book, a number of outstanding posts on the internet have contributed to the fundamental understanding of covenants and dispensations as they occurred throughout the Bible. In some cases, the source of material used was either unclear or unavailable. To those fellow Christians who have spent considerable time in composing biblical interpretation and meaning of the scriptures, I can only thank you for your wisdom and outstanding explanations of difficult concepts. You will know who you are and so will God.

I also wish to thank Alton Rogers of Aldersgate United Methodist Church in College Station, Texas for his encouragements, and several edits and helpful comments.

Special Thanks are Reserved For:

Candyce J. Phillips

Who proofed, edited and corrected the final draft of this manuscript

I am not ashamed: for I know whom I have believed, and am persuaded that he is able to keep that which I have committed unto him against that day.

Hold fast the form of sound words, which thou hast heard of me, in faith and love which is in Christ Jesus.

II Timothy 1:12-13

Table of Contents

The Eternal Plan of God

Dispensations-Covenants-Salvation

Study to show thyself approved unto God, a workman that needs not to be ashamed, rightly dividing the word of truth.   II Timothy 2:15

*Ask, and it shall be given you; **seek**, and ye shall find; knock, and it shall be opened unto you.*   Matthew 7:7

Introduction

The Authorized *King James Bible* consists of 66 different books, 1189 chapters and 31,102 verses. The Holy Scriptures are divided into two major sections: One called the *Old Testament* and the other called the *New Testament*. The Old Testament contains 39 books and the New Testament 27 books.

God, who at sundry times and in divers manners spoke in time past unto the fathers by the prophets, Hath in these last days spoken unto us by his Son, whom he hath appointed heir of all things, by whom also he made the worlds;   Hebrews 1:1-2

All scripture is given by inspiration of God, and is profitable for doctrine, for reproof, for correction, for instruction in righteousness: II Timothy 3:16

Every Christian is well-aware that the Holy Bible is divided into two main sections but sadly few fully understand the importance of the Old Testament. Most simply dismiss the Old Testament as irrelevant to the New Covenant Christian, or believe that it was a body of knowledge written to the Jews. Nothing could be farther from the truth. Jesus Christ quoted from the Old Testament 78 times. Almost every page of the Old Testament contains a prophecy, reference or type of Jesus Christ. It is impossible to fully understand all of the New Testament writings, particularly the books of Romans, Hebrews and Revelation, without understanding the Old Testament. The Apostle Paul, who wrote most of the New Testament, was well versed in Jewish customs and theology having studied under Rabbi Gamaliel I; who was perhaps the finest teacher of Old Testament Scriptures and Jewish Customs in the 1st century AD. The epistles of Paul are full of references to the Old Testament.

The Holy Scriptures contain both spiritual truths and a historical record of mankind from when the world was created (Genesis 1:1) to when the present world as we know it will end (Revelation 21:1). The Bible is often perceived as a scattered collection of stories, laws, promises, people, and guidelines for living. In reality, the entire body of scripture from Genesis to Revelation is a *progressive* and sequential record of how God has created, interacted, molded and dealt with mankind over a period of about 6,000 years. In 5 BC God sent His only begotten Son to this world to redeem all of mankind. The final act of redemption was played out on the cross of Calvary when Jesus Christ suffered, died and shed His precious blood to forgive the sins of the world in 30 AD. The opportunity for man to receive eternal life and permanent forgiveness of sins is now based upon believing that Jesus Christ is the Son of God, died on the cross of Calvary for our sins, and offers eternal life by faith and not by works. This *Dispensation of Grace* will terminate when the *ecclesia* or the *chosen ones* will be resurrected or raptured to meet Jesus Christ in the air. The work of redemption has been going on for about 2,000 years, and will continue until Jesus Christ returns again at His second advent. This study will examine almost 6000 years of recorded time and is divided into five different parts..

Part I: Overview of Dispensations and Covenants
Part II: The 7 Dispensations
Part III: The 8 Covenants
Part IV: Signs and Wonders
Part V: God's Eternal Plan of Salvation

Part I: Overview of Dispensations and Covenants

Dispensations

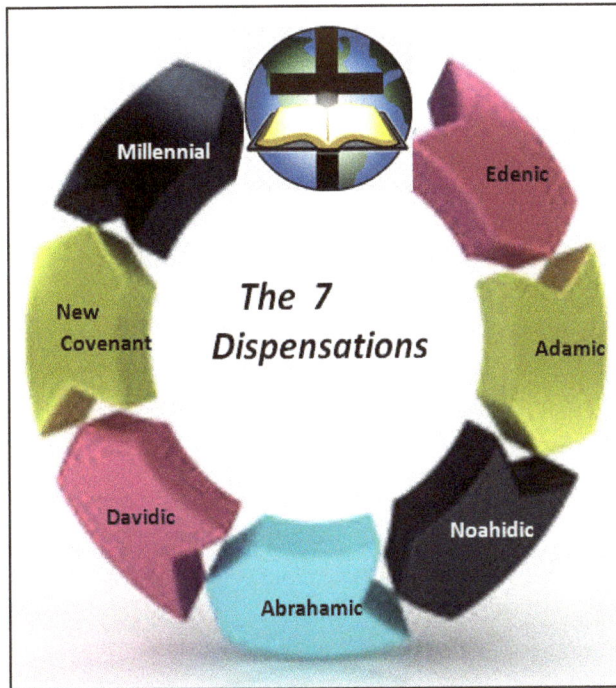

A *dispensation* is defined as a certain *period of time* during which God deals with people in a particular way. The Greek word for dispensation is *oikonomia*, and in the Bible it is used to mean a *manner, method, or particular arrangement of dealing with a group of people that God has chosen,* not the time period itself. Calling a dispensation primarily a period of time will not bear up under close scrutiny of the scriptures. Usually the length of time is not emphasized or even mentioned; it is the manner in which God is dealing with mankind over a particular period time which distinguishes one dispensation from another. The word **dispensation** is found four times in the scriptures, all in the New Testament writings of Paul (1 Corinthians 9:17; Ephesians 1:10, 3:2; Collosians 1:25). Each passage makes it clear that God is operating according to a specific promise, command, relationship or law. In Ephesians 3:2, God is redeeming man by *grace* and not by *works*. **Grace** is defined to operate not over a specific period of time but across all time. It is not a work-based doctrine but a principle. God revealed to all men that salvation was a free gift to all men, Jews and Gentiles alike. The appropriation of grace has always been based upon *faith* in His Son, Jesus Christ, and is a free gift. The Old Testament saints from Adam to the advent of Jesus Christ only knew that forgiveness of sins and redemption would someday come by a prophesied redeemer; New Covenant saints now know that the *anointed* or appointed one was Jesus Christ the Son of God. Salvation by faith has *always* been the only way that mankind could be redeemed from sin. In reality, it was not free at all but the price was paid for all mankind on the cross of Calvary.

The *Dispensation of Grace* can be contrasted with the *Dispensation of the Law,* where the relationship between man and God was based upon observing God's written laws and the Levitical sacrificial system. Under the Law, obedience was not an option but demanded. Obey the laws and live; break them and die (Galatians 3:10-13). The opposite of death is life, and Jesus Christ came not to abolish the law but to give life, both temporal and eternal. In the *Dispensation of Grace,* the law is still good because it was given to man by God, who is pure and good.

*And he (Christ) said unto him (the man who came to Him), Why callest thou me **good**? there is none **good** but one, that is, God: but if thou wilt enter into life, keep the commandments.* Matthew 19:17

Here Jesus is speaking to a Jewish man who recognizes that Jesus is the Son of God but does not understand how to achieve eternal life. Jesus answered unto him, *keep the commandments*. Christ is not telling the man that the only way to win eternal life is to *keep the commandments*; the man understood that this was impossible to do.

*For whosoever shall keep the whole **law**, and yet offend in one point, he is guilty of all* James 2:10
*For all have sinned, and come **short** of the glory of God* Romans 3:23

It is not that the Law was unjust and not good: salvation by grace did not supersede the law, but made it possible for all who believe in Jesus Christ as their savior to live and not die under eternal condemnation.

*For the **law** having a shadow of good things to come, and not the very image of the things, can never with those sacrifices which they offered year by year continually make the comers thereunto perfect.* Hebrews 10:1

We will have more to say about this later, but for now understand that God uses dispensations to deal with man in different ways, under different circumstances; to teach and reveal Himself and His eternal plans. When God reveals himself to man, the revelation may be at a specific point in time, but because it is the nature and character of God that is being revealed it is nether bound to that particular point in time or necessarily limited to the dispensation in which it is revealed.

The 7 Dispensations

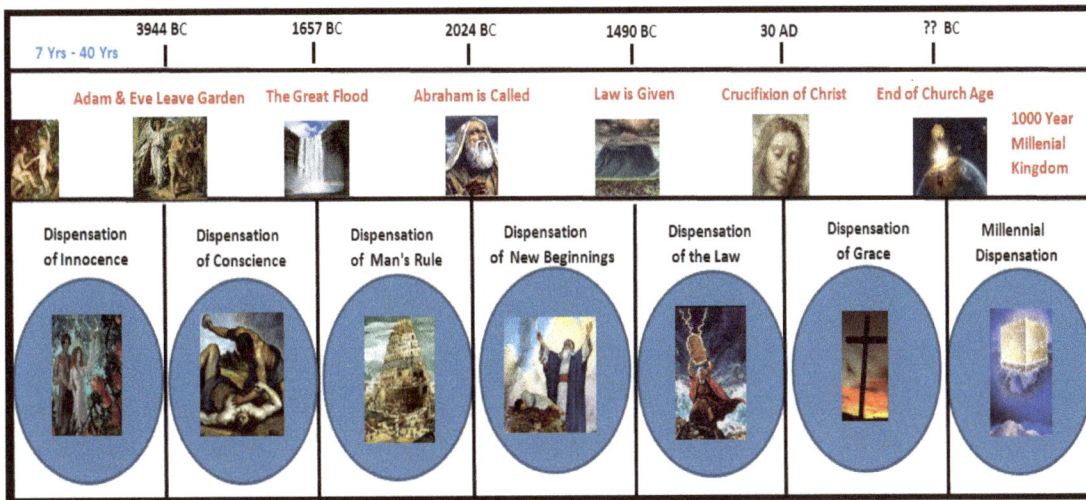

| 3944 BC | 1657 BC | 2024 BC | 1490 BC | 30 AD | ?? BC |
| 7 Yrs - 40 Yrs | | | | | |

| Adam & Eve Leave Garden | The Great Flood | Abraham is Called | Law is Given | Crucifixion of Christ | End of Church Age | 1000 Year Millenial Kingdom |

| Dispensation of Innocence | Dispensation of Conscience | Dispensation of Man's Rule | Dispensation of New Beginnings | Dispensation of the Law | Dispensation of Grace | Millennial Dispensation |

The history of man can be divided into seven different distinct periods of called *Dispensations*. The previous graphic provides an overview of the seven different dispensations that will be discussed in this book.

The study of dispensations is a method of interpreting history that divides God's work and purpose toward mankind into distinctly different periods of time. Different biblical scholars in different studies have identified between six and eight dispensations. In this book, we will examine seven different non-overlapping dispensations which can be clearly identified in the Biblical records. The seven different dispensations will be briefly described as follows. Each will be discussed in greater detail in Part II.

Dispensation of Innocence

The *Disposition of Innocence* began with the creation of Adam and Eve and continued until they sinned against God and were cast out of the Garden of Eden. The duration of this period of time is unknown. It has been proposed as one week, less than one year, seven years and even 40 years long by various biblical scholars.

Disposition of Conscience

The *Dispensation of Conscience* lasted about 1,656 years from the time that Adam and Eve were evicted from the Garden of Eden until the Great Flood (Genesis 3:8–8:22). This dispensation of time had no laws and the behavior of man was dictated by his own will and conscience. This dispensation demonstrates what mankind will do if left to his own will and conscience which have been corrupted by the inherited sin nature.

Dispensation of Man's Rule

The *Dispensation of Man's Rule* has also been called the *Dispensation of Human Government*. It lasted about 425 years and began when Noah and his family left the Ark after God had brought a great flood upon the whole earth. God looked at His creation and found that only Noah, his three sons and all their wives were worthy of saving; eight people in all. It is true that all mankind sprang from Adam and Eve, but it is equally true that people on the earth today also sprang from Noah and his family. Man was once again to re-populate the earth, and they ruled themselves without any written laws. They were ruled by their heart and their and own conscience. When man was left to follow his conscience after Adam and Eve were expelled from the Garden of Eden, they failed miserably. The Dispensation of Man's Rule ended when Abraham was called out of The Land of Chaldeans.

Dispensation of New Beginnings

The *Dispensation of New Beginnings* was 430 years long, and it was divided into two distinct periods of time: (1) The *Age of Promise,* and (2) The *Age of Bondage.*

> **The Age of Promise** lasted exactly 215 years. It began when God called Abraham out of Ur of the Chaldees, and ended when the Nation of Israel was berthed from Abraham's loins and became God's chosen people. The Nation of Israel grew and prospered, and they lived in the Land of Canaan until they left for Egypt during a great famine. During this period of time, God dealt with Israel as a *theocracy*; He was the divine ruler who directly communicated with man to reveal His sovereign will.

6

The Age of Bondage also lasted exactly 215 years. Because of
unbelief and failure to accept God as their theocratic ruler in Canaan,
the Children of Israel became a slave nation in Egypt. Israel spent
215 years in Egypt in slavery under several Egyptian Pharaohs.
Finally, God in His mercy heard their cries and sent His servant,
Moses, to lead them out of bondage. The Dispensation of Bondage
ended after the Nation of Israel crossed over the Red Sea and was
given the Law at Mt. Sinai.

Dispensation of The Law

The *Dispensation of the Law* lasted approximately 1520 years. It began at Mt.
Sinai in 1490 BC when Moses was given the 10 Commandments, and ended
when Christ suffered and died on the Cross of Calvary in 30AD. The
Dispensation of the Law is often called the *Old Covenant*. When it ended, it
was superseded and replaced by the *New Covenant*. The New Covenant
ushered in a new period of time called the *Dispensation of Grace*. The
Dispensation of Grace is still in effect today, and will continue until the 2nd
advent of Christ.

Dispensation of Grace

The Dispensation of the Law had one major feature: God gave Israel a set of 10
commandments to live by and 613 other commandments to govern their social,
dietary and religious life. The Law could never save anyone; it was a *taskmaster*
which brought man to the full realization that sin resulted in death and
condemnation. Our Lord and Savior Jesus Christ came not to destroy the Law
but to fulfill the law. His sacrificial death as the perfect Lamb of God on the
Cross of Calvary ended the Dispensation of the Law. Redemption from sin,
salvation, and eternal life was now based upon faith and appropriated by grace.
Salvation by faith and grace began what we now call the *New Covenant*. The
Dispensation of Grace started in 30AD and will continue until Jesus Christ
returns as a conquering king at His 2nd advent.

The Millennial Disposition

The seventh and final *Millennial Dispensation* will follow the Rapture of all
living saints and the resurrection of those who have died in Christ. This will be
accomplished at the second advent of Jesus Christ, and will be immediately
followed by the Wrath of God culminating in the final great Battle of

Armageddon. The Millennial Dispensation will last 1,000 years and is commonly referred to as the *Millennial Kingdom*. The end of the 1,000-year millennial kingdom will culminate in the creation of new heavens and a new earth. This earth as we now know it will be purged by fire and restored to an Edenic state; eternity will then begin.

Covenants

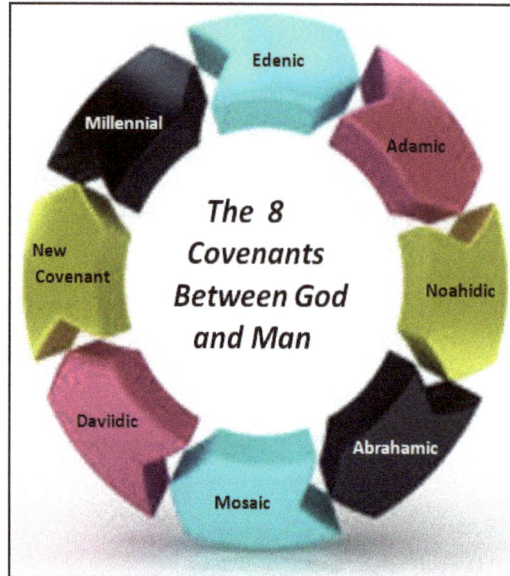

The seven Dispensations divide the full council of God's word into seven distinct periods of time. The seven Dispensations are not of the same duration, and they do not overlap with one another. Each Dispensation starts with a distinct event in which God will deal with man in a particular way. Equally important is the concept of a *Covenant Relationship* between God and mankind. **A covenant is a sacred agreement between God and a person or a set of people.** The Greek word for covenant can also mean *promise*. In this study we will examine 8 important covenants that God made with man.

When God makes a covenant agreement with mankind, there are always specific conditions and promises between the two parties. Man's relationship to God is always based upon one or more covenantal promises. The study of *Biblical Covenants* is central to understanding how God has dealt with man and the sin issue throughout the first six dispensations. Different dispensations always operate under specific covenant relationships with God, but not all dispensations are defined by covenants. Covenants between God and man can start and end *anywhere* across the spectrum of the seven dispensations which we will explain and discuss. Understanding the way covenants operate within and between the seven different dispensations will reveal to man how to *rightly divide the word of God.* Covenants between God and man fall into two mutually exclusive and independent categories. They are either (1) *Conditional,* or (2) *Unconditional.*

Conditional Covenants

A *conditional covenant* usually depends on the faithfulness of one or more parties, and the covenant is invalidated should one or both break the conditions of the covenant. Whenever a conditional covenant is made between God and man, if the covenant promises are made null and void the trespass is always made by man and not God. This is sometimes misunderstood; God will never invalidate or change the conditions of a conditional covenant, but He is justified in annulling the covenant if man fails to keep the conditions of the covenant.

Unconditional Covenants

An *unconditional covenant* is one that is not dependent on the faithfulness of either party, but remains valid from its point of initiation. Unconditional covenants are essentially unilateral between God and man. The interesting thing about an unconditional covenant between God and men is that no matter how unfaithful or disbelieving that man might be, the covenanting (promise) will always be fulfilled because God is faithful and true and cannot lie. What God promises He will fulfill. We will see that unconditional covenants initiated by God continue to be in effect from the moment God states His promises until the promises come true no matter how much time elapses. There may or may not be conditions to be met by man when God makes an unconditional covenant. Violation of those conditions may delay the fulfillment of the promise(s), but will not cancel the promise(s) of God.

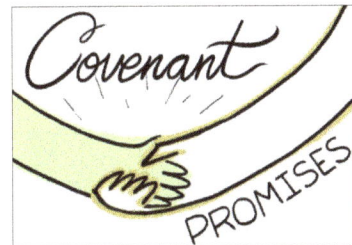

All covenants in the Bible between God and man are originated by God and are an act of His holiness and grace. Since God is faithful and true (Jeremiah 42:5), He cannot lie and cannot sin. Therefore, *conditional covenants* between God and man always terminate because of the unfaithfulness and the sinful nature of man. There were eight main covenants made between God and man throughout Biblical history.

- **The Edenic Covenant**
- **The Adamic Covenant**
- **The Noahidic Covenant**
- **The Abrahamic Covenant**
- **The Mosaic or Old Covenant**
- **The Davidic Covenant**
- **The Covenant of Grace or the New Covenant**
- **The Millennial or Kingdom Covenant**

The following diagram illustrates the timing and relationship between each of the seven different dispensations and the eight covenants which we will study. The key event which triggers each dispensation is also given, along with the approximate date that each of the seven dispensations begin and end. Except for the Davidic Covenant, the year in which each covenant is given corresponds to a dispensation start date. However, the duration of each covenant might span one or more dispensations if the covenant is unconditional.

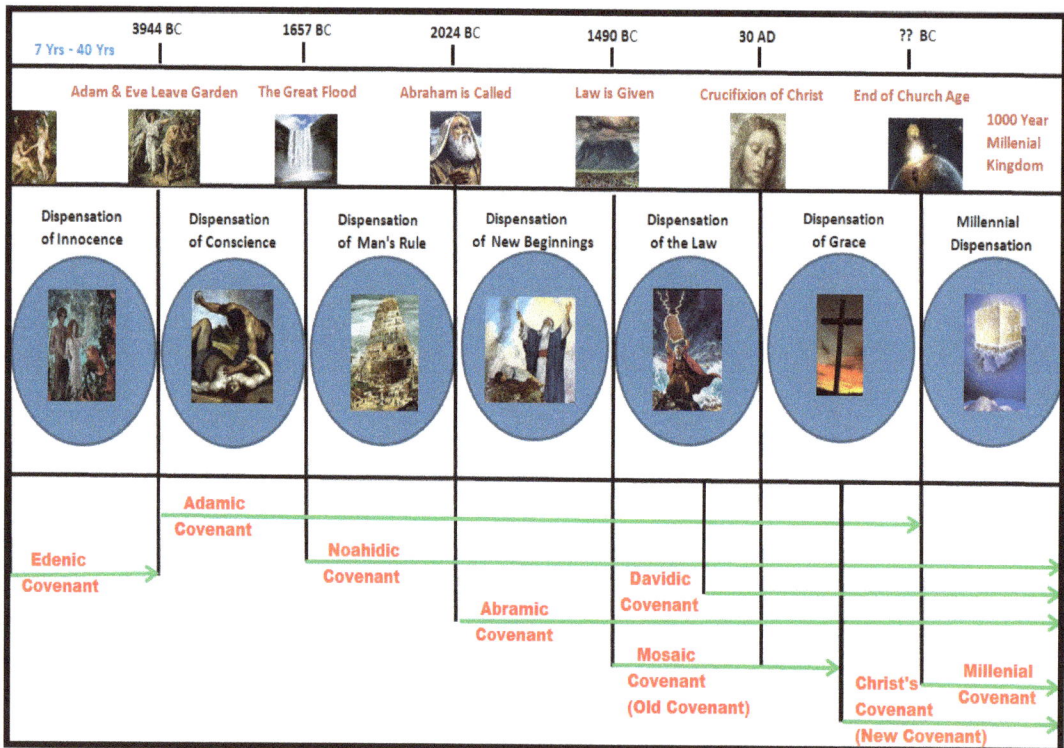

The Eight Covenants Between God and Man

The Edenic Covenant (Genesis 12:1-3)

God created the heavens and the earth in Genesis 1:1-31, and when He finished His creative work he said: *It was very good* (Genesis 1:31). The Lord then made man out of the dust of the earth; He called him Adam and then He created a beautiful place for him to live called the *Garden of Eden*. God decided that it was *not good for Adam to be alone*, so He made a woman called Eve starting with a rib from Adam. Adam and Eve lived in the Garden of Eden with all manner of animals; *And out of the ground made the LORD God to grow every tree that is pleasant to the sight, and good for food; the tree of life also in the midst of the garden, and the tree of knowledge of good and evil* (Genesis 2:9). God made the *Edenic Covenant* with Adam and Eve. He promised them that he would care for them, watch over them and keep them eternally young by providing a Tree of Life . Everything in the Garden of Eden was theirs to enjoy and use except for one thing: They were not to eat of the fruit of the Tree of Knowledge which stood in the midst of the Garden. This was the first covenant ever made between God and man, and it was conditional upon Adam and Eve obeying His only command to them. We know that both Adam and Eve disobeyed God and was cast out of the Garden of Eden. Hence, the first sin committed by man against God resulted in man tasting death and toiling by the sweat of his brow to live.

Adamic Covenant (Genesis 1:26-30, 2:16-17)

The *Adamic Covenant* was similar to the Edenic Covenant in that the word covenant is not actually used in the Genesis record. The Hebrew word for covenant means *promise*, and the Adamic covenant involved several promises between God and Adam & Eve. The Adamic Covenant was a set of conditions that God established for Adam, Eve and their offspring now that they were not living in the Garden of Eden. Man was cursed because they disobeyed God, and from that point on the ground would need to be cultivated and tilled. Thistles and thorns would also effect crop production. Eve was to experience pain in child-berth. The most severe penalty was that Satan would constantly be at *enmity* with mankind, bringing sickness and punishment upon mankind. How sad that Adam and Eve disobeyed and committed the first sin against God. Their act of disobedience continues to pit man against Satan today.

Noahidic Covenant (Genesis 9:11)

The first use of the word covenant in the scriptures occurs in Genesis 6:18. The actual covenant was given in Genesis 9:11. The *Noahidic Covenant* was spoken to Noah following the departure of Noah, his family, and all of the animals from the ark: *I (will) establish my covenant with you, that never again shall all flesh be cut off by the waters of the flood, and never again shall there be a flood to destroy the earth.* This covenant included a sign of God's faithfulness to keep His word; a rainbow would appear in the sky when it rained. This covenant was *unconditional* and did not depend upon the faithfulness of either Noah or his descendants.

Abrahamic Covenant (II Samuel 11:7-16, II Chronicles 17:10-14)

The Abrahamic Covenant was first made between God and Abraham in Genesis 12:1-3, and it was reinforced and expanded from Genesis 12 to Genesis 22. It was an extensive and far-reaching covenant between Abram (Abraham) and all of his offspring. We will discuss this later in much detail, but it contained four fundamental promises: (1) God pronounced a blessing upon Abraham, to make his name great and to make his seed into a great nation, (2) The covenant promised that Abraham's blessing would be extended to many people and nations. A blessing would fall upon all those who blessed Abraham and a curse would fall upon those who cursed him, (3) God vowed to bless the entire world through Abraham's seed; the fulfillment of this part of the covenant is through Jesus Christ, who was of Abraham's family line, (4) The fourth basic covenant was that Abraham's seed would be given what is now called the land of Canaan as a perpetual inheritance. This was an unconditional covenant.

The Mosaic Covenant (Exodus 20-Deuteronomy 28)

The *Mosaic Covenant* is sometimes called the *Old Covenant*. This was a *conditional* covenant found scattered between Exodus 20 and Deuteronomy 28. It promised the Israelites a blessing for obedience and a curse for disobedience. Much of the Old Testament chronicles the fulfillment of cycles of judgment for sin and blessings when God's people lost faith, repented and returned to God.

The Davidic Covenant (II Samuel 7:8-16).

The *Davidic Covenant* is actually a reassurance and expansion of the Abrahamic and the Mosaic Covenant. This *unconditional covenant* was given to King David, and reinforced the Land Covenant given to Abraham and his seed. This is sometimes called the Palestinian Covenant or the land Covenant. Neither is quite correct since the Davidic

Covenant involved more than just the land of Palestine, and the original Land Covenant was given to Abraham. Included in this covenant promise was the revelation that due to disobedience and unbelief, God would scatter Israel if they disobeyed God, but that they would eventually be restored to all the land of promise. This covenant will not be fulfilled until after the Jews, as a nation, turn to Jesus Christ as their promised Messiah during the great tribulation period described by the Apostle John in the Book of Revelation.

The New Covenant (Jer. 31: 31-34, Mat 26:28)

The *New Covenant* was made by Jesus Christ, the Son of God, at the Lord's Last Supper (Luke 22:20). The next day, he would be sacrificed on the cross of Calvary and through his sacrificial death He would take away the sins of the whole world (I John 2:2). The death of Christ confirmed the unilateral covenant promise that He made to Adam after Adam and Eve were cast out of the Garden of Eden (Genesis 3:15), and it fulfilled the words of Jeremiah the prophet (Jeremiah 31:31-34). Justification by forgiveness of sin was settled on the cross, and salvation was offered to the Jews by grace, and then to the Gentiles (Acts 14:44-52). The promise was first made to Israel then extended to everyone who comes to Jesus Christ in faith (Hebrews 9:15).

The Millennial Covenant

The *Millennial Covenant* is sometimes called the Kingdom Covenant. The Millennial covenant was actually spoken through a set of promises that occur throughout all of scripture, that prophesies of a 1,000-year dispensation that will immediately follow the Tribulation Period described in the Book of Revelation. The Kingdom covenant promises are found in many Old Testament and New Testament books. We discuss these promises as a separate covenant because of its significance in God's eternal plan for mankind.

Note: Do not confuse Holy covenants made between God and man with prophetic statements throughout the scriptures. Prophetic statements are made to individuals throughout the scriptures which reveal certain things which will take place. Covenants are broader in scope and time. We will distinguish between prophetic statements and covenants in Part III.

In Part II we will discuss some key events which took place in each of the seven Dispensations. A complete historical and Biblical treatment of the seven Dispensations in detail would require hundreds of pages and a discussion of the entire Bible. We have only presented some of the more important events through recorded time in the order in which they appear in the Holy Scriptures.

In Part III each of eight different covenants that God made with mankind are discussed within the context that they were put into place. It is certainly true that some might consider *any* command from God to mankind or any promise to punish man if they choose disobedience or sinful alternatives to the commands of God to also be a "covenant" . The eight covenants considered in this book have historically been considered a set of the most imprtant, far reaching and significant promises to man.

In Part IV of this book we consider a set of eleven visible and enduring signs and wonders which God has ordained for remembrance or temporal proof that He is both *omniscient* and *omnipotent*. One could argue that there are more or less than eleven signs to remind mankind that an important, sometimes cosmically significant, event has taken place, or a visible sign that a unique and singular event had or would take place but would never happen again.

The correct understanding of both Dispensations and Covenants as the history of man unfolds is crucial to understanding how God's purpose and plan was revealed throughout the ages. Once both have been clearly defined and discussed, in Part V of this book we will address the most important issue in man's plan for humanity: How each person is redeemed and saved throughout recorded time in each dispensation? This will be followed by answering a second intriguing question: What happened to every person that died in the Old Testament ?

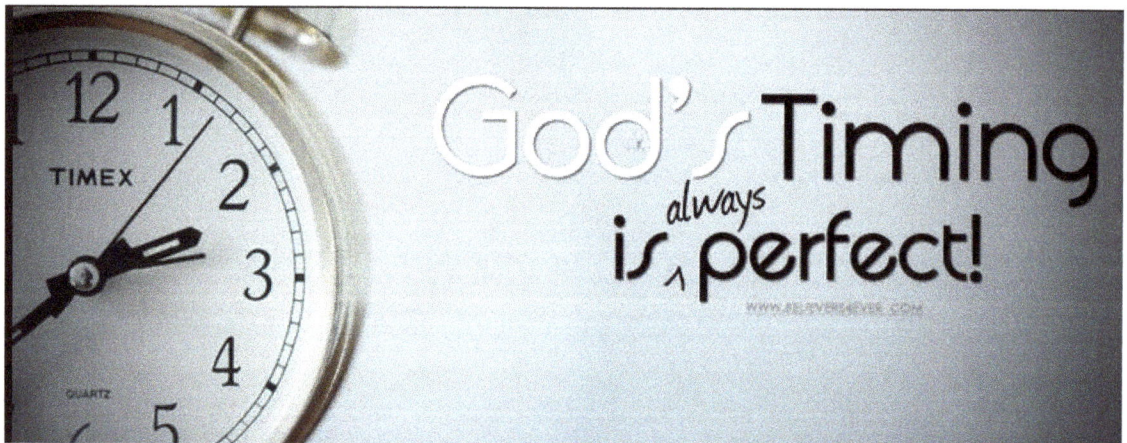

Part II: The 7 Dispensations of Recorded Time

The Dispensation of Innocence (Genesis 1:8-Genesis 3:8)

The Disposition of Innocence began with the creation of Adam and Eve, and continued until they were expelled from the Garden of Eden. The duration of this period of time is unknown. It has been proposed as one week, less than one year, seven years and even 40 years long. Although unknown, if Genesis 1 and Genesis 2 are carefully studied, it is evident that on day four God made the Sun and the Moon to determine night and day. One night (darkness) and one day (daylight) made up a single 24-hour day. On the fifth day the waters of the earth were populated and began to reproduce. On the sixth day the beasts of the earth, everything that grew in the earth and every bird and fowl that ruled the air were created by Jehovah. Finally, Adam was made on the sixth day; God's supreme earthly creation. It is obvious that every living creature, fowl and fish were created in six days, and Adam also. God rested on the seventh day, not because He was tired but because He had made the earth and everything on it which He had set out to do (Genesis 1:1-31). Now, where was Adam *after* he was created on the sixth day? He could NOT have been in the Garden of Eden, because the Garden of Eden was not created until Genesis 2:8, *after* God had finished His *creative* work. The earth and all of its varied terrain was not where God wanted to put Adam. God decided to give Adam a more suitable place to live. Adam needed a place where he could live and commune with God. *After* the seventh day was over, God created the Garden of Eden (Genesis 2:8) and placed Adam in its midst. Adam's first task was to meet and name every creature that lived upon the earth. This must have taken many days. In fact, it is implied that Adam became weary because he had no help (Genesis 3:20). Realizing that Adam needed a companion, God then created Eve for his mate (Genesis 2:18-22). The entire process would have had to have covered a much longer period of time; perhaps even a year. Adam and Eve were commanded to do five things while they were in the Garden of Eden.

> 1. Multiply and replenish the earth (Gen. 1:28).
> 2. Subdue (keep) the earth for their use (Gen. 1:28).
> 3. Exercise dominion over the animals, fowls and fish (Gen. 1:28).
> 4. Eat only fruit and vegetables which grew in the garden (Gen. 1:29).
> 5. Dress and keep the garden (Gen. 2:15).

We all know that it was Satan in the form of a serpent who deceived Eve. She then talked Adam into violating the only rule that God had imposed upon them which carried a penalty.

Of every tree of the garden thou may freely eat: But of the tree of the knowledge of good and evil, thou shall not eat of it: for in the day that thou eat thereof thou shalt surely die.
Genesis 2:16-1

One of the things that God commanded Adam and Eve to do was *to have dominion over all creatures that populated the earth.* It is proposed that Adam and Eve lived in the garden for some time and enjoyed the paradise that God had created for them. Finally, Eve was tempted by Satan and she believed his lie that if they ate of the Tree of the Knowledge of Good and Evil that they would now be like God. Adam and Eve both violated God's command and were cast from the Garden of Eden. If Eve had listened to this commandment, she might never have yielded to Satan in the form of a serpent. We have no scriptural record of how long Adam and Eve were in the Garden of Eden, but it seems when examining all the facts that it was not a few days as some propose but several months, perhaps even years. We cannot know how long the Dispensation of Innocence lasted, but it is really not important. It is only important to know that Adam and Eve existed in a pure state of innocence for some time before they disobeyed God and were cast out of the Garden of Eden. It is instructive to understand that God did not tempt Adam and Eve nor did he orchestrate the Fall of Adam. Man was created in innocence without any understanding of good and evil; everything was free and good. But when Adam and Eve fell to the lies of Satan and knew good from evil, evil (sin) became a reality. They inherently understood the difference in good (obeying God) and evil (disobeying God), and that when they disobeyed God they had become sinners. It is the most tragic act in the existence of mankind; from that point on, every living man and woman was born from the seed of Adam with the curse of sin upon their very existence. Adam and Eve were free to do anything they chose to do but eat of the Tree of Knowledge of Good and Evil. It is interesting that there was only *one* thing that they could not do. Who would imagine that with only one restriction on their existence that they would want to sin? Everything was free; they had to do no work, there was perfect climate and friendly animals to walk among. Such is the frailty and greedy nature of mankind.

It must be recognized that while God wanted to protect and love Adam and Eve, and provide for them everything they wanted and needed, He created both with the free will to choose who they would serve and obey: Satan or God. Paradoxically, the divine purpose of God in allowing Adam and Eve to fall to temptation is woven into the plan of redemption for mankind. If He would have interceded and vanquished Satan at that time, His supreme love and grace would not have been manifested through Jesus Christ. Man from that point on was aware of the penalties and degradation of choosing Satan over God. Man would need to recognize that he could never conquer the sin issue by himself. A Messiah called Jesus Christ was the only way to conquer sin from that point forward. Basic principles quickly arose which would remain in effect throughout all of the Ages:

1. **The wages of sin is death** (Romans 6:23).
   [16] *And the LORD God commanded the man, saying, Of every tree of the garden thou mayest freely eat: [17] But of the tree of the knowledge of good and evil, thou shalt not eat of it: for in the day that thou eatest thereof thou shalt surely die.*   Genesis 2:16-17

This is the first time that *death* is mentioned in the Holy Scriptures. What did God mean since Adam and Eve did not die but were simply cast out of the Garden of Eden? Adam and Eve were created to commune with God (Genesis 3:8) and to live forever, sustained by the Tree of Life (Genesis 2:9a). They wore no clothes (Genesis 2:25), but they were neither hot nor cold. The Garden of Eden was a perfect living environment. However, when Adam and Eve sinned they were given clothes and cast out of the Garden (Genesis 3:21-24). From that point on they no longer had access to the Tree of Life and all of the food in the Garden, but had to work for food by the *sweat of their brow* (Genesis 3:17-19). Created to live forever, man's days were now numbered. We are not told when Eve died, but Adam lived 930 years (Genesis 5:5). The average number of years that man would live has slowly decreased from that point in time. Because of their transgression, Adam and Eve also suffered spiritual death. This meant that they would die in sin, and that they could no longer live after death in God's presence. Adam and Eve and their children were separated from God both physically and spiritually. Were Adam and Eve ever redeemed from sin? We will discuss this later.

2. **The Innocence of Mankind was Gone Forever**
*The LORD knows the thoughts of man, that they are **vanity**.*   Psalms 94:11

When Satan deceived Eve, one of his lies had an element of truth to it. He told Eve: *your eyes shall be opened.* They were indeed opened, but what she saw would plague women

17

for the rest of time. Eve immediately recognized that she was naked, and in her shame she wanted clothes. Many women feel that they are not pretty, that they are overweight, that they need excessive makeup and that they are not loved because of their physical appearance; all are lies from Satan. God made each of us in His own image, and we should accept who we are. Just as Eve was made for Adam, there is an Adam for every Eve. Vanity can cause depression, social rejection and even suicide. The pristine and purity that Adam and Eve felt for each other was gone forever. So Adam and Eve made clothes out of fig leaves to cover their nakedness. Their nakedness was not so much physical as it was mental. Adam and Eve hoped that they could be concealed from God. Oh what mental torture must have resulted from one bite of fruit?

3. Mankind Could No Longer Approach God and Talk with Him Face to Face

God is Holy and cannot tolerate sin. Satan knew this, because he and 1/3 of all the angels were cast out of the Paradise of God because of rebellion and sin. We can well imagine that Satan reasoned that if he could cause Adam to sin, there would be no way that man or woman could be acceptable to God. He (Satan) did not understand or anticipate that God would send Jesus Christ to settle the sin issue 4,000 years later, and offer redemption to all those who would believe that He was the Son of God sent to save all mankind. When we look carefully at Romans 5:12, we find the devastating impact of Adam's sin. The curse on all men and women which is inherited from Adam would condemn mankind to the *sin nature* for the next 6,000 years or more. God only took two verses (Genesis 3:5-6) to record this terrible event.

Therefore, just as sin came into the world through one man, and death through sin, and so death spread to all men because all sinned.   Romans 5:12

.... because all sinned: Paul was saying that when Adam sinned, God knew that he would be the progenitor of all those who would come after him. All humanity was contained *in Adam* when he sinned, and so his sin was not merely individual, but corporate. When Adam sinned, it was actually imputed to the entire human race. Paul confirms this in Romans 5 and 1 Corinthians 15.

[18] *Therefore as by the offence of one judgment came upon all men to condemnation; even so by the righteousness of one the free gift came upon all men unto justification of life.*
[19] *For as by one man's disobedience many were made sinners, so by the obedience of one shall many be made righteous.*   Romans 5:18-19

[21] *For since by man came death, by man came also the resurrection of the dead.*
[22] *For as in Adam all die, even so in Christ shall all be made alive.*   I Cor. 15: 21-22

4. The Redemptive Plan of God is Revealed

After Adam and Eve sinned against God, the first prophetic words recorded in the Holy scriptures were spoken by God,

I will put enmity between thee and the woman, and between thy seed and her seed; it shall bruise thy head, and thou shall bruise his heel   Genesis 3:15

This is the first verse in the Holy Scriptures that speaks of a coming Messiah who we now know is Jesus Christ the Son of God. There have been many theological debates concerning the exact meaning of this prophecy. In Genesis 3:14, God is speaking to the *serpent*, who no doubt represents *Satan*. The first "thee" is Satan; the *woman* is directly referring to Eve, but almost certainly is also referring to all the subsequent offspring of women in the phrase "thy seed". In light of these observations, consider the following interpretation.

I will put hostility between Satan and Eve whom you deceived, and between the offspring of Satan's seed and the seed of Eve from which mankind will be birthed. The Messianic offspring of Eve shall bruise Satan's head, but Satan will bruise His heel.

There will be enmity (hostility and conflict) between his (Satan's) seed and her (Eve's) seed. God promised that eventually the serpent would *bruise the heel of the seed of the woman*. However, the seed of the woman would also *bruise Satan*. The Aramaic word for bruise can also mean *crush*. When Christ crushes Satan, he will be removed from this world (Revelation 20). This will be a fatal blow. Looking back through the ages of time, Satan has always been in conflict with God. There has also been constant conflict (warfare) between Satan and all the Old Testament saints who placed their faith in a coming Messiah (Jesus Christ), and since the crucifixion and resurrection of Christ, this conflict continues between Satan and all the New Testament saints who believe upon His name. Christ was born in the flesh by Mary (Eve's seed). His heel was bruised on the Cross of Calvary, but by His sacrificial death He *crushed* Satan. Christians of faith today have the Holy Spirit to help us, and Satan no longer has dominion over our lives.

*Ye are of God, little children, and have overcome them: because **greater** is he that is in you, than he that is in the world.*   I John 4:4

5. Timeless Bliss in the Garden of Eden is Replaced by Recorded Time

After Adam and Eve were deceived by Satan, the Age of Innocence transitioned into time as we now know it. Measurable time in terms of years can be traced from when Adam and Eve left the Garden of Eden until the present time by following biblical clues. The most popular and well-known construction of time was published by Archbishop James Ussher (1581–1656), who determined that the world was created on Saturday, October 22 in 4004 BC and that Adam and Eve were driven from the Garden of Eden on Monday, November 10, in 4004 BC. Ussher's proposed date of 4004 BC differed little from other estimates, such as those of Jose ben Halafta (3761 BC), Bede (3952 BC), Scaliger (3949 BC), Johannes Kepler (3992 BC) and Sir Isaac Newton (4000 BC). The year in which God created the earth is nothing more than fiction, since there is no biblical record of exactly when this occurred. However, the history of mankind can be traced from when Adam and Eve were cast out of the Garden of Eden to the crucifixion of Christ by carefully studying the scriptures. This year has been determined by Phillips (Biblical Chronology from Adam to Christ) as 3944 BC, and will be used to estimate Dispensational time periods in this book. The *duration* of each dispensation except the Dispensation of Innocence would likely be the same regardless of when the first year started.

The Dispensation of Conscience (Genesis 3:9-Genesis 8:14)

The *Dispensation of Conscience* lasted 1,656 years from the time that Adam and Eve were evicted from the Garden of Eden until the Great Flood. This period of time can be determined with confidence using the genealogies in the Book of Genesis 5:1-7:6 (Phillips). This dispensation had no written law and the behavior of man was dictated by his own will and conscience. In the previous *Dispensation of Innocence*, Adam and Eve had no knowledge of good or evil. They only knew the goodness of God, and they had complete freedom to do as they saw fit. Without the knowledge of good and evil, everything was good. The only thing prohibited by God was not to eat of the fruit which grew on the tree of knowledge of good and evil.

[16] *Of every tree of the garden thou may freely eat:*
[17] *But of the tree of the knowledge of good and evil, thou shall not eat of it: for in the day that thou eat thereof thou shall surely die.*   Genesis 1:16-17

Since Adam and Eve were innocent and did not understand the difference between good and evil, they created in their own mind what was evil and what was good. This gives rise to *self-judgment* in which each individual decides right from wrong, which may or may not coincide with the will of God. There is an old saying that *one should let your conscience be your guide*. This is only true if your conscience reflects truth, love and honesty and is guided by the word and character of God. That is why after Jesus Christ nullified the curse of the law, He sent to us the *Holy Spirit* to guide our conscience. It should be understood that knowledge of good and evil carries with it *responsibility* to follow the good and righteous path. Inherent in this responsibility is the *choice* to choose between good and evil, and flee from Satan. If Eve had fled from Satan and rejected his lies, both Adam and Eve would not have fallen. It all fairness, when Satan appeared to Eve and deceived her, this was before she fully comprehended the difference between good and evil; what Satan promised her might have been very pleasing to her innocent nature. However, the crux of the matter was *not* that she (and Adam) believed Satan's lies, it was that they both chose to disobey God when they ate of the fruit. Whether she was fully able to distinguish good from evil when she was tempted was not the problem; she deliberately and willfully disobeyed God (Genesis 2:16-17). When she ate of the fruit, she immediately understood what she had done but it was too late. Understanding that both she and Adam had done evil, they both sought to hide from God but it was too late. From that moment on, the offspring of Adam and Eve were able to understand the difference between good and evil. Since there was no written law, each person had to distinguish what was good and what was evil, and whether or not to follow God's commands based upon the conscience and free will of each individual.

It has since been true throughout recorded time that even if man has not heard of the true YHWH God, and he has no written laws to guide his moral and social behavior, that he has within his own heart the notion of what is right from what is wrong. Man inherently can distinguish good from evil, and has a moral structure which can decide whether to actually do good or to do evil. The prime example of this is Cain and Abel. When Cain killed his brother Abel, he immediately knew he had sinned and challenged God by saying *Am I my brother's keeper?* (Genesis 4:9). This rebellion was inherited from Adam and Eve as a result of them doing the one thing that God had forbidden them to do, eat from the tree of Knowledge of Good and Evil. Because Adam and Eve disobeyed God and committed the first sin, it was this one act that cursed everyone who would follow. Every person born after the fall has the original sin nature upon them. Man (and woman) is born into this world with an inherited desire to sin upon their mortal flesh. This is why Christ had to be conceived of woman by a supernatural act. Only God could produce an offspring which was sinless at birth. It is because of the Adamic curse that Adam was called the "first man" and our Lord and Savior Jesus Christ was called a "quickening spirit" and "the last Adam".

[22]   *For as in **Adam** all die, even so in Christ shall all be made alive.*
[45]   *And so it is written, the first man **Adam** was made a living soul; the last **Adam** was made a quickening spirit.*   I Corinthians 15: 22, 45

The *Dispensation of Conscience* demonstrates what mankind will do if left to his own will and conscience, which have been tainted by the inherited sin nature.

We see sin being manifested not long after Adam and Eve were cast out of the Garden of Eden. Cain slew Abel, and tried to hide his act from the Lord. But of course, the Lord already knew what Cain had done. The story will not be retold here of how this all ended. What is important is that *there was no written law against murder.* So what sin did Cain commit?

For until the law sin was in the world: but sin is not imputed when there is no law.
     Romans 5:13

Just because there was no written law against murder and deception (lying) when Cain killed his brother Abel does not mean that Cain did not sin against God.

[9] And the LORD said unto Cain, Where is Abel thy brother? And he said, I know not: Am I my brother's keeper? [10] And he said, What hast thou done? the voice of thy brother's blood crieth unto me from the ground.   Genesis 4:9-10

Recall that in Genesis 4 both Cain and Abel brought an offering to the Lord. Cain brought an offering of fruit from the ground, and Abel slaughtered a lamb and offered it to the Lord. The offering of Abel was acceptable to the Lord, and the offering of Cain was unacceptable to the Lord. Here we have dramatically illustrated why this is called the *Dispensation of Conscience.* Cain knew in his own conscience that he had done wrong; no written law was needed. The first act of Cain which led to his downfall was that he was *jealous* of his brother. In a fit of jealously and rage, he committed the first murder recorded in the bible. The second act of Cain demonstrated that he had no love in his heart: *am I my brother's keeper?* The third act of Cain was to lie to God about what he had done: *Where is your brother?* and Cain replied *I know not.* These three acts of rebellion revealed the true nature of Cain; he had sinned but exhibited no remorse or sorrow, only arrogance. But there were no written laws that commanded: love thy brother as thyself; Thou shall not lie; Thou shall not commit murder. It is recorded in Genesis 4:16 that *Cain went out* (was driven out) *from the presence of the Lord* because of his sins. Sin and disobedience always results in separation of man from God. The only path to reconciliation and total forgiveness is through His Son, Jesus Christ. Adam was alive at this time, and he undoubtedly had told both Cain and Abel that salvation from their sin(s) would be through a promised Messiah who would arise from his seed. The acts of Cain were no doubt fueled by Satan. Satan also knew that a Messiah would arise from the loins of Adam, and that if he could destroy Abel by death and Cain by sin, then the Messiah could not arise. But God will not be mocked or deceived. He had Adam and Eve birth a man of God named *Seth.* It was through Seth and his progeny that Christ would arise (Luke 3:38).

Seth had a son called *Enos* or Enoch (weak or frail) who was also in the linage of Christ. The scriptures record that at that time, *men began to call on the name of the Lord* (Genesis 4:26). Scholars are divided upon the true meaning of Genesis 4:26. Some say that man began to worship the Lord and turn to Him for divine guidance; others say that this means that man began to create graven images and worship them in the name of the Lord. It is likely that the latter interpretation is correct. This has been true through all recorded biblical history. After the fall, in the ancient world prior to Noah, only one man is recorded in the Bible to have *walked with the Lord* (Genesis 5:22), and it was Enoch (Hebrews 11:5). Enoch, the seventh from Adam, is the son of Jared through the lineage of Seth (Genesis 5:3-18). ....*and Enoch walked with God after he begat Methuselah* (Genesis 5:22). Enoch fathered Methuselah who lived the longest life of any known human (969 years), and Methuselah sired *Lamech*. Enoch knew God, and he never tasted death.

*And **Enoch** walked with God: and he was not; for God took him*   Genesis 5:24

Enoch was translated to heaven shortly before God flooded the earth. Perhaps God knew that he was old and could not survive long. Many scholars say that Enoch is being reserved in a special place so that he can witness for Jesus Christ during the tribulation period yet to come (Revelation 11). In 1056 BC Noah was born to *Lamech*. Noah lived to be 950 years old, but when he was 600 years old, God saw that man had become evil and unrighteous. The pinnacle of rebellion against God came when a group of angelic creatures came upon the earth and took wives among the women to themselves. The result was a race of giants which were called **Nephilim.** They were the offspring of the "sons of God" and the "daughters of men" in Genesis 6:4. Why would angelic beings do such a thing? The angels who caused this rebellion were fallen angels sent directly from Satan. As when Cain slew his brother Abel, Satan was trying to disrupt the ancestral line of Jesus Christ by contaminating the entire human race. Of course, God put down this rebellion by casting all these angelic creatures into a place of darkness where they remain today awaiting the final judgment (Jude 6).

After Satan attempted to corrupt mankind, man had no problem in turning away from God and rejecting Him on their own. Finally, man became so wicked that God decided to take an unbelievable path of total destruction; He decided to bring a great flood upon the earth that would destroy every living creature that roamed the earth except for Noah and his immediate family, and every animal that was saved by entering Noah's ark,

And God said unto Noah, The end of all flesh is come before me; for the earth is filled with violence through them; and, behold, I will destroy them with the earth. Genesis 6:13

God said to Noah that He had looked at His creation and found only Noah, his three sons and all their wives *righteous* (Genesis 7:7). Because of Noah and his righteousness, Noah and his family were saved from drowning; eight people in all. Genesis 6:3 records that God *destroyed the earth*. This is a poor translation of what actually took place. God did not completely destroy the earth but he did destroy every living creature that remained on the earth. The exception was all of the sea and fresh water creatures. The environment was much different in those days. Most biblical researchers believe that the earth was like a greenhouse surrounded by a canopy which protected them from harmful rays, and most biblical scholars believe that it had never rained before the flood. The rivers, streams and plant life were perfectly sustained by a mist which fell upon the earth in the cool of the evening.

Some argue that this mist eliminated the need for rain until the time of the flood. The basis of this claim is Genesis 2:5–6 where it is written that before the sixth day of the seven-day Creation Week, God had watered all of the plants with a mist, and that He had not yet caused rain to fall. However, presence of the mist while Adam and Eve lived in the Garden of Eden does not preclude the existence of or the need for rain after they were cast from the garden of Eden. The conjecture that rain did not fall until after the Flood has no real biblical support. It is more likely that since Adam and Eve had no clothes to protect them until after they disobeyed God, they lived in a greenhouse-like environment in the garden of Eden which was perfect for their continued existence. In any case, God became so displeased with the descendants of Adam and Eve that He decided to send rain and drown all mankind except Noah and his family.

And God said unto Noah, The end of all flesh is come before me; for the earth is filled with violence through them; and, behold, I will destroy them with the earth. Genesis 6:3

God flooded the entire earth by releasing all atmospheric water and all subterranean water upon the earth at the same time.

In the six hundredth year of Noah's life, in the second month, the seventeenth day of the month, the same day were all the fountains of the great deep broken up, and the windows of heaven were opened. Genesis 7:11

It rained upon the earth relentlessly for 40 days and 40 nights, and then the rain from heaven ceased. After 365 days Noah found dry land on Mt. Ararat, and Noah and his family emerged from the great ark which saved them and many animals from death and destruction. Noah and his family entered into a new, purified world. This ended the *Dispensation of Conscience* and initiated the *Dispensation of New Beginnings.*

The Dispensation of Man's Rule (Genesis 8:15-11:22)

The Dispensation of Man's Rule was similar in structure to the Dispensation of Conscience.

Dispensation
of Man's Rule

(1) They both started with only a few humans.
(2) They both had access to a new, pristine world.
(3) Both were not led by any written law, but by their conscience.
(4) God spoke directly to man and dealt with mankind on a personal basis.
(5) Both Adam & Eve and Noah and his family were told to replenish the earth.
(6) In both dispensations God gave man dominion over the animal kingdom.
(7) Both dispensations were well aware of both the grace of God and the potential Wrath of God.

However, there were also significant differences in both dispensations.

(1) After the Flood, man had to deal with environmental issues such as rain, hail and tornadoes. This necessitated that man had to build houses and wear seasonal clothes.

(2) Men in the Dispensation of Conscience were vegetarians; in the Dispensation of Man's Rule they were allowed to eat meat, but not blood (Genesis 9:4-5). Since Cain and Abel, the significance of blood was understood to be a part of the sacrificial rituals, but was not yet linked to the redemption of sins. It was not until the Written Law of God came to Moses and the Children of Israel that blood was to become the symbol of redemption and salvation (Numbers 17-19).

> *For the life of the **flesh** is in the blood: and I have given it to you upon the altar to make an atonement for your souls: for it is the blood that maketh an atonement for the soul.*   Leviticus 17:11

(3) Although man was allowed to govern themselves, some moral laws were needed to be spoken by God. To keep man from destroying themselves, God instituted capital punishment for the crime of murder (Genesis 9:6). This was a direct consequence of Cain murdering his brother Abel. For some reason known only to God, he did not kill Cain but exiled him to a life of toil and strife. Within government and social units, man was given free will to choose God or mammon and all societies would have the power of life and death.

The *Dispensation of Man's Rule* lasted about 425 years. It began when Noah and his family left the Ark, and it ended when Abraham was called out of the Land of Chaldees.

Men were left to follow their conscience after Adam and Eve were expelled from the Garden of Eden, and they failed miserably. In reality, one could call the Dispensation of Man's Rule an extension of the Age of Conscience because the written law was not given to man until after the Exodus from Egypt at Mt. Sinai. However, one major difference was that until Adam and Eve ate of the fruit and were able to distinguish good from evil and disobeyed God, there had been no sin in the world. When Adam and Eve were banished from the Garden, they now had the sin nature and God in His mercy gave them oral instructions on how to live; there was no written laws.

Noah and his family were commanded to walk in righteousness and to *be fruitful and multiple upon the earth* (Genesis 8:17). All mankind has descended from the loins of Noah, but Noah inherited the original sin from Adam so everyone is born with a sin nature. Noah and his descendants did multiply, and *by these were the nations divided in the earth after the flood* (Genesis 10:32). There are no details given as to how *the nations were divided*, but it appears that the sons and daughters of Noah formed their own clans and settled across the known earth in social groups. Social groups demand social structure, so it was at this time that man began to develop the concepts of self-governance.

It is not likely that the descendants of Noah actually settled in the Western Hemisphere, but they probably did roam and settle around the western and northern shores of what is now called the Mediterranean Sea, and *the whole earth was of one language* (Genesis 11:1). As time passed, these descendants of Noah began to forsake the God of their fathers and turned to idol worship and all kinds of immoral acts. Man is inherently decidedly wicked.

[28] And even as they did not like to retain God in their knowledge, God gave them over to a reprobate mind, to do those things which are not convenient;
[29] Being filled with all unrighteousness, fornication, wickedness, covetousness, maliciousness; full of envy, murder, debate, deceit, malignity; whisperers.   Rom. 1:28-29

About 350 years after the flood things came to a place of abomination that even the Lord in all of His mercy could not tolerate. Descendants of Noah and his sons led by *Nimrod* migrated to the Land of Shinar which was near the site of modern day Babylon, southeast of where the Garden of Eden was located. There they determined to *be like God* and build a great ziggurat called the *Tower of Babel* to reach into the heavens. As a result of this rebellion, God in His wrath confounded their language and scattered them all throughout all the earth.

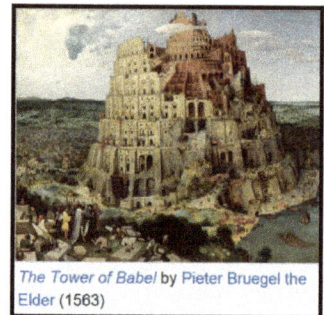

The Tower of Babel by Pieter Bruegel the Elder (1563)

[7] let us go down, and there confound their language, that they may not understand one another's speech.
[8] So the LORD scattered them abroad from thence upon the face of all the earth.
        Genesis 11:7-8

Scientists, archeologists and linguistic experts have long attempted to explain how civilizations in North America, Africa and other places like the Yucatan Peninsula evolved with different languages, colors and customs. In spite of obvious differences, all emerged with many similarities across great distances. For example, most nations separated by the Atlantic and Pacific oceans record in their history stories of a great flood. All can be explained easily by faith in God's Holy Word. God created different languages and enforced His own command to fill the earth. The result was the rise of different languages, nations and cultures. From that point on, human governments have evolved to various stages of democracy, socialism and communism.

The Lord had brought His Wrath and His sovereign control upon mankind at Babel, but He was not through with His creation. God will always preserve a faithful remnant that He will use to carry out His divine purpose. Grace was displayed in the third dispensation when God chose and preserved His remnant. The particular remnant God anointed and chose after the flood are the people whose names are listed in Genesis 11:10-31. These names trace the genealogy of Noah all the way down to Abraham, through whom God would bring about the *Dispensation of New Beginnings*. In spite of the great flood and scattering the people at Babel, God did preserve a family line to fulfill His promise of a *righteous seed* which He made to Adam. As man began to evolve and follow after other gods and idols, YAWH God approached a man after His own heart called Abram.

The Dispensation of New Beginnings (Genesis 12:1 , Exodus 18:27)

The *Dispensation of New Beginnings* lasted exactly 430 years (Exodus 12:40, Galatians 3:17). It began when God called Abraham out of Ur of the Chaldees (Genesis 12:1) and ended when Moses received the Law from God at Mt. Sinai after he had led the Children of Israel out of Egyptian bondage. It will be discussed in two parts, both of which lasted 215 years. The *first* began when Abram left Ur of Chaldees and ended when Jacob left Canaan to live in Egypt. The *second* began when Jacob arrived in Egypt and ended when God delivered His people from bondage and gave the written law to Moses at Mt. Sinai. The Dispensation of New Beginnings was different from both the Dispensation of Man's Rule and the Disposition of Innocence. God had promised Adam and Eve that a savior would arise who would *bruise Satan's head*, but there were no details given concerning how this might occur. All that was known was a redeemer would arise out of the *seed* of Eve. God now revealed more about the coming Messiah. God promised Abraham that through his seed the entire world would be blessed and that the long-awaited Messiah would arise from his family line to redeem all mankind. This demonstrates that the word of God is characterized by *progressive revelation* through divinely revealed truth. God also made a land Covenant with Abraham which we will discuss later in Chapter 3. It was revealed that the land of Canaan would be perpetually given to Abraham and his offspring, but not immediately.

Dispensation of New Beginnings

(1) In this disposition, God revealed that the Messiah would come out of the loins of Abram (Abraham).
(2) God will choose the land of Canaan for His chosen people to live, grow and multiply into a great nation.
(3) The nation which God calls forth will be called Israel.

(4) Israel will be divinely preserved and protected even though they will lose faith and migrate to Egypt. They will be in bondage under the Egyptian pharaohs until they once again turn to God.

(5) God will hear their cry and lead them out of Egypt using His faithful servant Moses.

The Dispensation of *New Beginnings* consisted of two sequential, non-overlapping periods of time: The *Age of Promise* and the *Age of Bondage*.

The Age of Promise lasted exactly 215 years. It began when God called Abraham out of Ur of the Chaldees, and ended when Jacob and his family migrated to Egypt. They had prospered and grew in the land of Canaan until they left for Egypt during a great famine. During this period of time, God dealt with Israel as a theocracy. He was the divine ruler who directly communicated with man to reveal His sovereign will.

The Age of Bondage also lasted exactly 215 years. Because of unbelief and failure to accept God as their theocratic ruler in Canaan, the Children of Israel became a slave nation in Egypt. Israel spent 215 years in Egypt in slavery under a series of Egyptian Pharaohs. God heard their cries and sent His servant Moses to lead them out of bondage. The Age of Bondage ended when the nation of Israel crossed over the Red Sea and was given the Law at Mt. Sinai.

The Age of Promise

The *Age of Promise* began when God called Abram at age 75. Abram was living with Noah when God called him forth to leave for the land of Canaan (Book of Jasher, Chapter 9). His father was *Terah*. Terah was the chief administrative officer for Nimrod, who ruled over Babylon. Terah was an idol worshipper and a pagan.

Abram spent his younger days living in the house of Noah who taught Abram to worship the one true God. Noah died when Abram was age 58. Abram continued living with Noah's son *Shem* in Noah's house until he was called to the Land of Canaan.

[1] *Now the LORD had said unto Abram, Get thee out of thy country, and from thy kindred, and from thy father's house, unto a land that I will shew thee:*
[2] *And I will make of thee a great nation, and I will bless thee, and make thy name great; and thou shalt be a blessing:*
[3] *And I will bless them that bless thee, and curse him that curseth thee: and in thee shall all families of the earth be blessed.*

30

[4] *So Abram departed, as the LORD had spoken unto him; and Lot went with him: and Abram was seventy and five years old when he departed out of Haran.* Genesis 12: 1-4

When Abram left for Canaan, He took with him his nephew, Lot, his wife Sarai and possibly an unknown number of other people with him. This was before Abram was renamed Abraham by God, and his wife Sari was renamed Sarah.

And Abram took Sarai his wife, and Lot his brother's son, and all their substance that they had gathered, and the souls that they had gotten in Haran; and they went forth to go into the land of Canaan; and into the land of Canaan they came. Genesis 12:5

Abram and Lot settled near Bethel and remained there for many years. A famine came upon the land, and Abram left Canaan to go to Egypt. It was here that the first sin of Abram was recorded in scripture; Abram's wife Sarai was very beautiful and fearing that the Pharaoh of Egypt would kill him for his wife, Abram called Sarai his sister. Sure enough, the Pharaoh took Sarai into his house as a concubine. God sent plagues upon the Pharaoh and after a short period of time he called Abram to him and Abram confessed his lie. The Pharaoh banished Abram and his family from Egypt and he returned to Bethel.

After Abram moved to Canaan, the Lord came to him and established three covenants: (1) *land*, (2) *seed*, and (3) *blessings*. They are confirmed and reconfirmed several times between Genesis 10 and Genesis 15.

[2] *And I will make of thee a great nation, and I will **bless** thee, and make thy name great; and thou shall be a **blessing**:*
[3] *And I will bless them that bless thee, and curse him that curse thee: and in thee shall all families of the earth be **blessed**.* Genesis 12:2-3

[14] *And the LORD said unto Abram, after that Lot was separated from him, Lift up now thine eyes, and look from the place where thou art northward, and southward, and eastward, and westward:*
[15] *For all the **land** which thou see, to thee will I give it, and to thy seed for ever.*
[16] *And I will make thy **seed** as the dust of the earth: so that if a man can number the dust of the earth, then shall thy seed also be numbered.*
[17] *Arise, walk through the **land** in the length of it and in the breadth of it; for I will give it unto thee.* Genesis 13:14-17

When God met with *Abram* He made a covenant with him, ratified the covenant with animal sacrifices, and renamed him *Abraham* (Genesis 17:5) which *means father of many.*

[5] *Neither shall thy name any more be called Abram, but thy name shall be Abraham; for a father of many nations have I made thee.*
[6] *And I will make thee exceeding fruitful, and I will make nations of thee, and kings shall come out of thee.*
[7] *And I will establish my covenant between me and thee and thy seed after thee in their generations for an everlasting covenant, to be a God unto thee, and to thy seed after thee.*
[8] *And I will give unto thee, and to thy seed after thee, the land wherein thou art a stranger, all the land of Canaan, for an everlasting possession; and I will be their God.*
[9] *And God said unto Abraham, Thou shall keep my covenant therefore, thou, and thy seed after thee in their generations.*   Genesis 17:5-9

There are many things which occurred throughout the Dispensation of New Beginnings. We will not discuss them all, but several important events will be briefly discussed.

Abram and Lot Separate

Abram and Lot prospered but Lot's herds and flocks were too great to flourish with those of Abram; so Lot journeyed to the Land of Sodom and Gomorrah which was a land of wickedness. Several pagan kings, led by the King of Sodom attacked Lot and his family, took them captive, and seized all of his possessions. Hearing of Lot's misfortune, Abram came to the rescue of his nephew and rescued him and all of his possessions. It was upon his return to Canaan that we are introduced to the mysterious King of Salam, Melchizedek.

Melchizedek

Abram had not only rescued Lot and restored all of his flocks and possessions, but he had also conquered several kings and kingdoms who had fought against him (Genesis 14:1-7). So Abram returned to his own land with Lot and all of the spoils of war. Upon returning Abram encountered a man called Melchizedek, the King of Salem. Melchizedek, whose name means *King of Righteousness,* was a King of Salem (Jerusalem) and priest of the Most High God. He is referenced only four places in the scriptures: Genesis 14:18–20, Psalm 110:4, Hebrews 5:6-11, and Hebrews 6:20-7:28). The sudden appearance and disappearance of Melchizedek in the book of Genesis is somewhat mysterious. Melchizedek and Abram met after Abram's defeat of King Chedorlaomer and his three allies. Melchizedek presented bread and wine to Abram and his weary men, and he then bestowed a blessing upon Abram in the name of *El Elyon* (God, Most High). He next praised God for giving Abram the victory (Genesis 14:18–20). It is interesting to note what Abram did next. He gave Melchizedek an offering of 10% of everything that he had taken when he rescued Lot. The reader should easily recognize that this event took place long before the Law was given to Moses. The *tithe* of 10% provides the New Covenant Christian with a guideline of how much tithe should be given today. In the Dispensation of Grace, there is no written requirement of how much to tithe. Certainly, the concept of tithing is well rooted in each church today. The figure of 10% is often preached in the pulpit today, but the truth is that the only guideline of how much a New Covenant Christian should tithe is given by the Apostle Paul.

[6] *But this I say, He which soweth sparingly shall reap also sparingly; and he which soweth bountifully shall reap also bountifully.*
[7] *Every man according as he purposeth in his heart, so let him give; not grudgingly, or of necessity: for God loveth a cheerful giver.*   II Corinthians 9:6-7

The choice of how much an individual should return to God in terms of a tithe is strictly up to one's own conscience. The New Testament nowhere commands, or even suggests, that Christians submit to a legalistic tithe system. The New Testament nowhere designates a percentage of income a person should set aside to support the work of the kingdom. In this author's opinion, a 10% tithe is a good percentage to use in love, because Abram gave to Melchizedek 10% without any written requirement. The New Testament talks about the importance and benefits of giving. We are to give as we are able. Sometimes that means giving more than 10 percent; sometimes that may mean giving less. It all depends on the ability of the Christian and the needs of the church. Every Christian should diligently pray and seek God's wisdom in the matter of participating in tithing and/or how much to give. Above all, any tithe or offering should be given with pure motives and in an attitude of worship. Why would 10% be a good guideline? It is because that Melchizedek was clearly a shadow and type of Jesus Christ.

We read in Hebrews 6:19-20 that Jesus Christ, after His resurrection, became a High Priest in heaven *after the order of Melchizedek*. What does this mean? Several things are made evident by the author of Hebrews. *First*, Melchizedek was the King of Salem. *Salem* means *peace*, so Melchizedek was called the *King of Peace*. Christ is the *Prince of Peace*. *Second*, we understand from the scriptural accounts, that both Melchizedek and

Jesus Christ were called Priests of the *Most High, God*. The proper interpretation of this identification is that both were placed into that position of authority by God. *Third*, Melchizedek was said to have no beginning and no ending, just like Jesus Christ. Some expositors have postulated that Melchizedek was the pre-incarnate Christ. This is preposterous. What would Christ be doing in Salem acting as an earthly king? Hebrews 7 also settled this conjecture.

[14] *For it is evident that our Lord sprang out of Judah; of which tribe Moses spake nothing concerning priesthood.*
[15] *And it is yet far more evident: for that after the similitude of Melchizedek there ariseth another priest,*
[16] *Who is made, not after the law of a carnal commandment, but after the power of an endless life.*
[17] *For he testifieth, Thou art a priest for ever after the order of Melchizedek.*
　　　　Hebrews 7:14-17

Fourth, both Melchizedek and Messiah were called a king and a priest. This could only happen in a Dispensation not governed by the Law, because under the Law given to Moses no one could serve as a king *and* a priest, not even King David. Recall the consequences of King Saul usurping the function of Samuel in 1 Samuel 13. Under the New Covenant, anyone who has been born again and has accepted Jesus Christ as their Lord and Savior is no longer under the law, and like Melchizedek will reign as both kings and priests throughout the 1,000-year Millennial Kingdom:

And (He) *hath made us kings and priests unto God and his Father; to him be glory and dominion forever and ever. Amen.*　　　　Revelation 1:6

Ishmael is Born

Abram is perhaps the most revered patriarch in the Jewish religion because of his obedience and faith in God. When God made His covenant with Abram, he was 75 years old and Sarai his wife was about 65 years old. After 10 years had passed, Abram and Sarai his wife had still produced no offspring. In an act of disbelief, Sarai decided to take matters into her own hand. Knowing that she was now past 75 years old and Abram was well past 85, she doubted if she would ever conceive. So Sarai offered her handmaiden, Hagar, to Abram to bear his child. Abram consented, and Hagar bore a son called *Ishmael*. Ishmael was not the son of promise but one born out of an adulterous relationship. The result would prove disastrous, for Ishmael spawned the nations of Iran, Iraq and others in the Middle East.

Sodom and Gomorrah

After Abram sired Ishmael, the wickedness of Sodom and Gomorrah came into remembrance before the Lord and stirred up His Wrath. The story of Sodom and Gomorrah is recorded in Genesis 19. Sodom and Gomorrah were two cities in close proximity to one another, possibly contiguous and separated in name only. Lot had moved to Sodom with his family, and one day he was visited by two angels disguised as men. Lot invited them to stay in his house. That evening the *men* of Sodom and Gomorrah approached his house and insisted upon having sex with the *two strangers.* The two disguised angels smote the crowd with blindness; and told Lot that he, his wife and his two daughters must leave early the next day because God was going to destroy the city(s) with *fire and brimstone.* The sin which prompted God to destroy Sodom and Gomorrah is very clear: it was *homosexuality.* The incident gave rise to the term *sodomy,* and Sodom and Gomorrah were always to represent complete depravity and sinfulness. As Lot left the city by divine instruction, he was told that neither he nor any member of his family should look back on the destruction. Lot's wife did look back and God turned her into a pillar of salt.

There are some who refuse to condemn homosexuality or lesbianism as a sin; they claim that it is genetic; however, the story of Sodom and Gomorrah clearly teach otherwise. There are those who say that homosexuality is not even mentioned in the New Testament, but they show their ignorance of scripture by making this claim.

Even as Sodom and Gomorrah, and the cities about them in like manner, giving themselves over to fornication, and going after **strange flesh***, are set forth for an example, suffering the vengeance of eternal fire.*   Jude 7

The term "strange flesh" has been grossly misinterpreted by the homosexual community. The following commentary is offered as biblically correct by the theologian John Gill.

> *... going after strange flesh; or "other flesh"; meaning not other women besides their own wives, but men; and designs that detestable and unnatural sin, which, from these people, is called sodomy to this day; and which is an exceeding great sin, contrary to the light of nature and law of God, dishonorable to human nature, and scandalous to a nation and people, and commonly prevails where idolatry and infidelity do.*   John Gill, Bible Exposition

The Age of Bondage

The second new beginning or the *Age of Bondage* started when, after a long famine in Canaan, Jacob moved his family and Abraham's descendants from Canaan to Egypt. This departure from Canaan was a direct act of disobedience and lack of faith. Jacob died 17 years later and the nation of Israel became a slave to the Pharaoh of Egypt. They would remain in bondage for another 198 years making bricks out of mud and straw to build the Egyptian pyramids.

In 1060 AD God had appeared to Abram and told him to go to the land of Canaan where He would bless him and his seed. Abraham prospered and he and his offspring remained in Canaan for 215 years until he lost faith in God and a great famine drove them into Egypt. There they became a nation of slaves to the Egyptian Pharaohs for another 215 years. But God had not abandoned His *chosen people* (Genesis 12:1-22); He heard their cries and sent His servant Moses to lead them out of bondage. The *Dispensation of New Beginnings* ended when the nation of Israel crossed over the Red Sea and was given the Law at Mt. Sinai.

The Dispensation of The Law

The Dispensation of the Law began at Mt. Sinai in 1490 BC when Moses was given the 10 Commandments, and ended when Christ suffered and died on the cross of Calvary in 30 AD. Moses led the people out of Israel after 10 plagues were brought against the Pharaoh and Egypt. The 10th plague brought the *Angel of Death* upon all of Egypt killing every firstborn of man and animals which were not divinely protected by the blood of the first Passover Lamb. The Pharaoh's firstborn son was killed by the Death Angel

Dispensation of the Law

and he finally relented, releasing the children of Israel from bondage and slavery. Moses led the people to Mt. Sinai, and 50 days after leaving Egypt God gave them the 10 commandments and a set of other laws to govern their social, dietary and religious lives. This is commonly called the *Law of Moses*, but it is in fact the *Laws of YHWH*. Most Christians will readily recognize and know the 10 commandments, but there are 613 laws which God gave to Israel. The nation of Israel would be a *Theocracy*, with the Levitical Priesthood, Aaron, and Moses serving as intermediaries between God and Man.

Almost immediately, the Children of Israel rebelled against God, and after the disbelief of 10 spies sent to reconnoiter the Promised Land, they were condemned to a total of 40 years wandering in the wilderness before they would be allowed to enter the Land of Promise across the Jordan River. The Dispensation of the Law contained many remarkable events.

1. The Children of Israel became a New Nation under God when it emerged from the Red Sea after God had destroyed the army of the Pharaoh. They were free from the bondage of Egypt and were ready to inherit the land of Canaan, which had been promised to Israel in a covenant with both Abraham and King David.

2. The nation of Israel arrived at Mt. Sinai 50 days after leaving Egypt, and received the Law from God through His servant Moses.

3. God also gave Israel a set of 613 other laws to govern their social, religious and dietary behavior and appointed Aaron and his sons (Levites) to serve as a royal priesthood.

4. The Levitical sacrificial system was initiated to provide atonement for sins in the Tabernacle of Moses.

5. After receiving the Law, the children of Israel marched to Kadesh-barnea where Moses sent 12 men to spy the land. After finding giants in the land, the spies returned with a bad report, all except Joshua and Caleb. As punishment for their lack of faith, God declared that Israel would wander in the wilderness for another 38 years (40 years in all) and that every male alive at that time would die in the wilderness except for Caleb and Joshua. Even Moses would die without entering into the Land of Promise (Canaan) for disobeying God and striking a rock to bring water instead of speaking to the rock (Numbers 20:8-12).

6. Joshua led Israel as Commander-in-Chief across the Jordan River, and after a seven-year period of conquest, conquered all opposing forces with the Angel of the Lord and the Ark of the Covenant leading them on.

Joshua moved the Ark to Shiloh, divided the land among the tribes of Israel, and the land was settled.

7. Due to apostasy and lack of faith, the nation of Israel lived in the land but wars never ceased. They never fully settled the land promised to Abraham or King David.

8. The height of power came under King David who united and expanded the kingdom, and under King Solomon his son.

9. King Solomon, who started so well, fell into apostasy and sin and after his death the United Kingdom was divided into two separate kingdoms: the Northern Kingdom called Israel and the Southern Kingdom called Judah.

10. When the Northern Kingdom fell to the Assyrian Empire in 932 AD, 10 of the original tribes were taken into captivity and were never heard from again. We call these the *Ten Lost Tribes of Israel*.

11. When the Southern Kingdom of Judah fell to Nebuchadnezzar and the Babylonian Empire in 586 BC, the rest of the original 12 tribes were deported to Babylon.

12. After 70 long years of exile, a remnant of Israel was allowed to return to Jerusalem. This began a long period of 400 years called the *years of silence*.

13. Finally, Herod the Great rebuilt Solomon's Temple and allowed the Jews to re-establish the Levitical sacrificial system.

14. In 26 AD, Christ came to the River Jordan to be baptized by John the Baptizer, and began His 3.5-year ministry of reconciliation.

15. The Dispensation of the Law ended on Nisan 14, 30 AD on the Feast of Passover, when Jesus Christ the Son of God was crucified on the Cross of Calvary. The Old Covenant and the Dispensation of the Law had passed away, and the New Covenant or the Dispensation of Grace began.

The Dispensation of the Law, which is often called the *Old Covenant* was superseded and replaced by the *New Covenant*. However, the concept of a New Covenant was not new at all. It was prophesied by the prophet Jeremiah over 1200 years earlier.

*They are turned back to the iniquities of their forefathers, which refused to hear my words; and they went after other gods to serve them: the house of Israel and the house of Judah have broken my **covenant** which I made with their fathers.*   Jeremiah 11:10

Behold, the days come, saith the LORD, that I will make a new covenant with the house of Israel, and with the house of Judah: Not according to the covenant that I made with their fathers in the day that I took them by the hand to bring them out of the land of Egypt; which my covenant they brake, although I was an husband unto them, saith the LORD: But this shall be the covenant that I will make with the house of Israel; After those days, saith the LORD, I will put my law in their inward parts, and write it in their hearts; and will be their God, and they shall be my people. Jeremiah 31:31-33

The *Dispensation of the Law* lasted 1520 years but God was not through with his chosen people. After 400 *years of silence* in which there was *no prophet in Israel* God instituted His final and perfect redemptive plan for all mankind; Jews and Gentiles alike.

The Dispensation of Grace

The sixth dispensation is the *Dispensation of Grace* or the *New Covenant* . It began on the Feast of Pentecost in 30 AD when Christ suffered and died on the cross of Calvary. His sacrificial death as the pure and perfect Lamb of God issued in a new era in which salvation was offered to Jews and Gentiles alike by grace, and not by works. The Dispensation of Grace is still in effect today, and will continue until the second advent of Christ.

Malachi is the last book written in the Old Testament, and it was compiled in about 430 BC. It closed the writings of God which we now call the *Old Testament.* Malachi was a post-exilic book, meaning it was written after the return from the 70-year Jewish exile in Babylon. Malachi was the last prophet in the Old Testament, and the Book of Malachi is prophetic in nature. Malachi addressed the sins of the people and the corruption of the Levitical priesthood. He then prophesied that a man (John) would arise which would prepare the way for the long-awaited Messiah of Israel (Malachi 1-3). In a great sweep through time, he spoke in the last chapter of the Old Testament about the inevitable and terrible *Day of the Lord,* which will come and in which the *proud and the wicked* will burned up like *stubble* leaving neither root nor branch. The 400 years between when Malachi finished prophesying and Christ was born are called the *years of silence*; because *there was no prophet in the land.* All that we know of that period of time is from non-biblical, historical writings, including the *Works of Josephus* who was a Jewish historian.

The Dispensation of the Law actually came to a close in 26 AD when John the Baptizer looked up and said: *Behold the Lamb of God, which taketh away the sins of the world* (John 1:21). It was Jesus Christ, the Son of God, who had arrived to draw every man and woman to Him who believed in faith

*And he (Abraham) believed in the LORD; and he counted it to him for **righteousness**.*
      Genesis 15:6
*But without **faith** it is **impossible** to please him*   Hebrews 11:6

Christ initiated His 3.5-year ministry to the Jews to fulfill the covenant promises which were spoken to all of the Old Testament prophets, and to live a sinless life under the Law. After the Jews corporately rejected Christ and failed to accept Him as the long-awaited Jewish Messiah of promise, the Old Covenant passed away and the New Covenant began. Salvation is now available to all, Jews and Gentiles alike. The sacrificial death of Christ as the perfect Lamb of God ushered in salvation by grace and faith, by which all sinners past and present could be justified, sanctified and glorified.

For by one Spirit are we all baptized into one body, whether we be Jews or Gentiles, whether we be bond or free; and have been all made to drink into one Spirit.
      I Corinthians 12:13

[21] *But now the righteousness of God without the **law** is manifested, being witnessed by the **law** and the prophets*
[27] *Where is boasting then? It is excluded. By what **law**? of works? Nay: but by the **law** of faith.*
[28] *Therefore we conclude that a man is justified by faith without the deeds of the **law**.*
      Romans 3:21, 27-28

The *Dispensation of Grace* began with the sacrificial death of Jesus Christ on the Cross of Calvary which ended the Old Testament sacrificial system forever. The Son of God was the perfect Lamb of God. He who knew no sin became sin for the whole world. The New Covenant and salvation by faith rests in Christ's blood (Luke 22:20). The eternal blessings which await all believers were guaranteed by the resurrection of our Savior from the grave after 3 full days and 3 full nights. Salvation is obtained by *faith*, and appropriated by *Grace*. The redeeming grace of Jesus Christ and His precious blood flowed all the way back to Adam and Eve and forward to His second advent. The work on the cross extends salvation forward to every believer Jew or Gentile, that will live during the church age. His sacrificial death as a man and as the Son of God forgave the sins of all of the Old Testament saints who died in faith. Man's responsibility during the *Dispensation of Grace* is to believe in Jesus, the Son of God (John 3:18), and to follow after Him and His commandments. In this dispensation the Holy Spirit indwells in all believers as the *Pericles* or the *Holy Spirit*. (John 14:16-26). This dispensation has lasted for over 2,000 years, and no one knows when it will end. We do know that it will end when the fullness of the Gentiles has arrived. The following truths must be understood by all believers in the present age.

First, Adam and Eve were created in innocence and lived in the Garden of Eden without the sin nature. When both entered into sin, they not only disobeyed God's command but they brought about death, despair, catastrophes, wars, hatred, bigotry, lies, evil and idolatries of all kinds upon mankind. This is because the *sin nature* was imputed to all mankind through the seed of Adam. This demanded that a Messiah would need to arise who would redeem all mankind and take away their sin(s). *Second*, it must be understood that the Messiah promised to all Old Testament saints was Jesus Christ, the Son of God. When He chose to suffer and die on the cross of Calvary, He took upon Himself the sins of the world, past, present and future. By that one sacrificial act, all men and women, past and future) would be saved by *faith*. The issue of sin was settled once and for all, and the permanent forgiveness of sin is now *justified* by the blood of Jesus Christ as the sacrificial Lamb of God. It important that the concepts of justification, sanctification and glorification are well understood.

> **Justification** - being *declared* perfect, a single act of Grace by God to the repentant sinner
> **Sanctification** - the process of *seeking* holiness and perfection in Christ, a day-by-day activity by God and the Holy Spirit working in and through each born-again Christian
> **Glorification** - *becoming* perfect, the moment when the struggle is over, when heaven is entered and God awards you with a new body and a new, sinless life

Justification and Sanctification follows a person accepting Jesus Christ as their personal Savior and being *born again*. Justification is imputed to each born-again believer by grace. Sanctification is a life-long journey for each Christian as they follow after Christ. Glorification and eternal life in Christ is *obtained* by faith, *appropriated* by grace, and *accomplished* by Jesus Christ. When Christ settled the sin issue at the cross, salvation became so simple that even a child could understand.

For God so loved the world, that he gave his only begotten Son, that whosoever believeth in him should not perish, but have everlasting life.   John 3:16

Sometime in the future, Christ will return again and when He does, He will: (1) resurrect everyone who has accepted Him as Lord and Savior and died in faith, (2) rapture out both Jews and Gentiles alike; who are alive and live by faith. (3) defeat Satan and all of His forces at the Battle of Armageddon. Following the last great battle at Armageddon, the Jewish believers who have accepted Christ as their long-awaited Messiah will populate the land promised to Abraham and King David during the 1,000-year millennial kingdom. This period of time is the prophesied *Millennial Dispensation*. New Covenant believers who had died in faith or who were alive at the Rapture of the Body of Christ are destined to serve as a Royal Priesthood during the new Millennial Kingdom with Christ (I Peter 2:9).

The Millennial Dispensation

The seventh and final *Millennial Dispensation* will immediately follow the *Rapture* of all living saints: the *resurrection* of all those Old and New Testament saints who have died in Christ, the *second advent of Jesus Christ*, and the final great *Battle of Armageddon*. It will last 1,000 years and is commonly referred to as the *Millennial Kingdom*. The end of the 1,000-year millennial kingdom will culminate in the creation of new heavens and a new earth; the earth will be restored to an Edenic state. Christ and all of the saints will rule and reign for 1,000 years. King David will sit again upon his throne in the City of Jerusalem, and the nation of Israel will physically inherit and live in the Land of Promise. It will be a glorious age in which Satan will be bound in the bottomless pit for 1,000 years. Incredibly, sin will once again abound since mankind and the land are still under Adam's curse. After the 1,000 years are over, Satan will be released from his prison and assemble all of the unrighteous to just outside of Jerusalem for the final battle. The end will come swiftly as Jesus Christ will vanquish Satan and all of his followers. Following this last battle, God will purify and cleanse the earth by fire and a New Heaven and a New Earth will emerge. Christ will then rule and reign forever in the New Jerusalem.

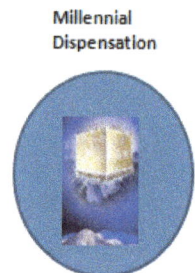

Millennial
Dispensation

Part III: The Covenants

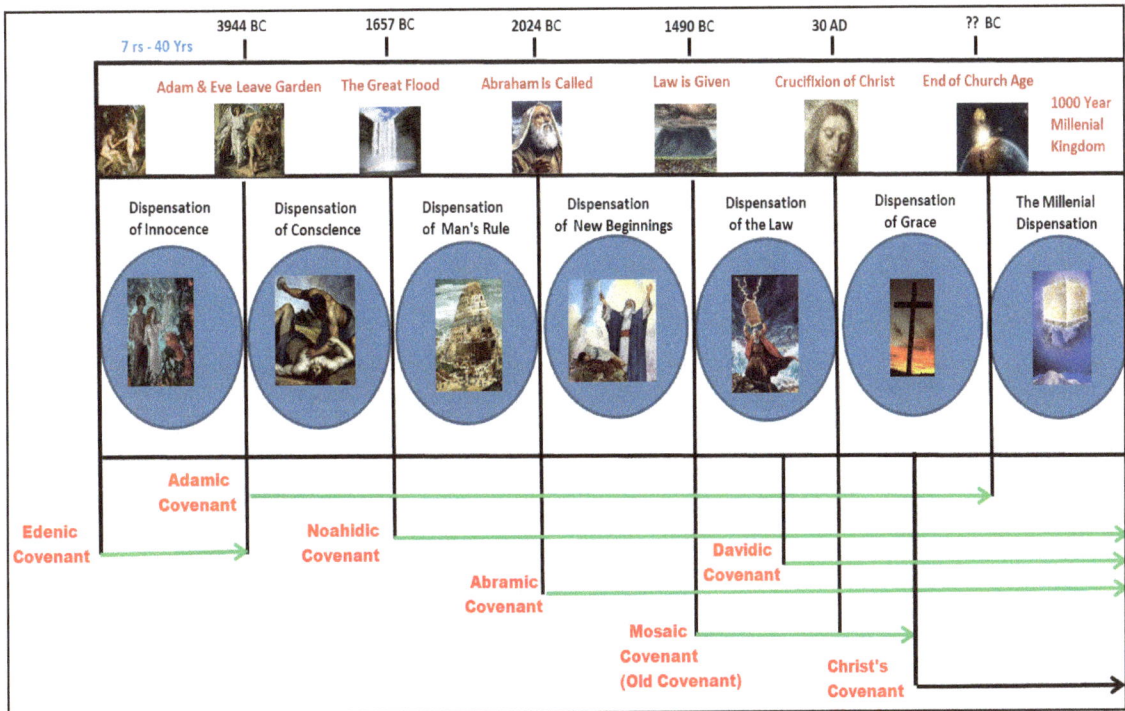

The Seven Dispensations discussed in Part II divide the existence of mankind into seven non-overlapping periods of time. Each dispensation represents a distinct era in which God has dealt with man in a different way. Another way to describe and categorize how God has dealt with man is through the *covenants* that God has made as time has progressed from when Adam was created and placed in the Garden of Eden until Christ ascended to Heaven in 30 AD. According to Webster's Dictionary, a covenant is a *formal, solemn, and binding agreement between two or more parties.* A covenant is also a solemn *promise.* In Scripture we see two different types of covenants that God makes with men: *Conditional* and *Unconditional.* An unconditional covenant is one which God will keep regardless of man's actions. The promise that God makes is not conditioned upon any action or pledge being kept by man as time goes on. By breaking a covenant with God, man will always suffer consequences and might fall out of God's favor for an undetermined amount of time, but if God has said He will do something in an unconditional covenant He *will* do it at some point in time. An example of an unconditional covenant is the land covenant that God made with Israel. A *conditional* covenant made between God and man is not binding if one party breaks the terms of the

43

covenant. If the covenant is violated, the terms and promises of the covenant are made null and void. An example of a conditional covenant is that which was made between Adam and Eve & God.

There is usually a severe punishment involved if man breaks a covenant with God, often stated in the original agreement between the two parties. Man must obey the terms of the covenant in order to receive the promises related to it. In the context of this study we are only concerned with covenants made between God and man. We will identify *eight* covenants which God has made with man. Each one has a time element which begins and ends at a particular point in time. In all cases, we will know when a covenant began but we may not know exactly when it might end. An example of this uncertainty is again the unconditional land covenant made to Abraham and later reiterated to King David. The land covenant with King David began when he ruled as King of Israel, but will not be fulfilled until the Millennial Kingdom begins.

The Edenic Covenant

The first Covenant relationship that God initiated with man is called the *Edenic Covenant*. It was made with Adam & Eve in the Garden of Eden. The word *covenant* is not found in God's instructions to Adam before the fall, but God made *conditional* promises to Adam and Eve which we will call the Edenic Covenant; they are recorded in Genesis Chapter 1.

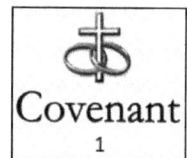

Covenant
1

[28]And God blessed them, and God said unto them, Be fruitful, and multiply, and replenish the earth, and subdue it: and have dominion over the fish of the sea, and over the fowl of the air, and over every living thing that moveth upon the earth.
[29] And God said, Behold, I have given you every herb bearing seed, which is upon the face of all the earth, and every tree, in the which is the fruit of a tree yielding seed; to you it shall be for meat.
[30] And to every beast of the earth, and to every fowl of the air, and to everything that creepeth upon the earth, wherein there is life, I have given every green herb for meat: and it was so.   Genesis 1:28-30

The Edenic covenant had the following general conditions.

- Mankind (male and female) were created in God's image.
- Adam and Eve would have dominion (rule) over the animal kingdom.
- A directive to Adam and Eve was to reproduce and inhabit the entire Earth.

- Mankind was to be vegetarian (eating of meat was not permitted until the Noahic covenant (Genesis 9:3).
- Eating the fruit of the tree of the knowledge of good and evil was strictly forbidden.

The Lord had told Adam that he was to dwell in the Garden of Eden and commanded him to *dress and keep it* (Genesis 2:15). Adam was to reign freely over the Garden of Eden and would never need to work or till the soil to eat or be nourished.

Of every tree of the Garden of Eden, thou shalt freely eat   Genesis 2:16

However, this covenant or promise to Adam had one exception.

But of the tree of the knowledge of good and evil, thou shall not eat of it: Genesis 2:17

This was a *conditional covenant* between God and Adam, because Adam was required to obey the terms of the covenant in order to not suffer the consequences of breaking it. Although theologians debate how many promises were made to Adam, the prohibition to not eat of the fruit of the tree of good and evil constituted the main Edenic Covenant. What was the penalty placed upon Adam and Eve when they broke the Edenic Covenant?

[16] Unto the woman he said, I will greatly multiply thy sorrow and thy conception; in sorrow thou shalt bring forth children; and thy desire shall be to thy husband, and he shall rule over thee.
[17] And unto Adam he said, Because thou hast hearkened unto the voice of thy wife, and hast eaten of the tree, of which I commanded thee, saying, Thou shalt not eat of it: cursed is the ground for thy sake; in sorrow shalt thou eat of it all the days of thy life;
[18] Thorns also and thistles shall it bring forth to thee; and thou shalt eat the herb of the field;
[19] In the sweat of thy face shalt thou eat bread, till thou return unto the ground; for out of it wast thou taken: for dust thou art, and unto dust shalt thou return.   Genesis 3:16-19

In addition, Adam and Eve would be cast out of the Garden of Eden forever. The most devastating penalty for disobedience would be physical death.

for in the day that thou eatest thereof thou shalt surely die.   Genesis 2:17

The force of Genesis 2:17 was not immediate death, because Adam lived for 930 years after he was cast out of the garden. The implication is that like all mortal men, from the moment that life begins outside of the woman's womb the body begins to age and die. Adam lived much longer than men and women today, because he began life in a perfect garden environment with no sickness, sin or physical decline. He was created to live forever and commune with God in the cool of the evening (Genesis 3:8). It should be understood that in the Edenic state, Adam was not aware of either good or evil. Everything was perfect and good; there was no concept or knowledge of evil. The concept of sin may not have been clearly understood, but Adam and later Eve were no doubt very clear that disobedience to God and the violation of their covenant would lead to punishment. Adam and Eve would die if they ate of the *fruit* of the *Tree of Good and Evil.*

It must also be recognized that even if sin was not clearly defined, when Adam and Eve disobeyed God they created the first sin against God. The entire human race sprang from Adam's seed, and since Adam had taken on the sin nature, all who would follow from his loins would be born into that same sin nature. Man cannot redeem himself from acts of sin and so Adam understood after the fall that there must arise a Messiah who would not only take away his sin but the sins of his progeny. That Messiah would come over 4,000 years later and would be called *Jesus.* The first prophecy given in the Holy Scriptures concerned this coming Messiah can be found in Genesis 3.

And I will put enmity between thee and the woman, and between thy seed and her seed; it shall bruise thy head, and thou shalt bruise his heel. Genesis 3:15

The Edenic Covenant was highly significant for several reasons. The fall of Adam and Eve established a pattern to be repeated throughout the Scriptures: (1) man sins, (2) God judges sin, (3) God punishes those who willingly sin, and (4) God shows His mercy and grace by predicting that a Messiah would arise to take away the sins of the world. All covenants between man and God show us that sin *always* has consequences. These consequences are either physical, spiritual or both. Understanding the different covenants in the Holy Scriptures and their relation to each other is important in understanding God's covenantal relationship with His chosen people. We will clearly see that God establishes different covenants with man at different points in time for only one reason: to place man into an intimate relationship with Him. As we will see in Section IV, they also reinforce and form His plan of redemption as revealed in Scripture. This was the purpose of placing Adam and Eve in the Garden of Eden, choosing the nation of Israel as God's chosen people, and sending His only Son to earth to save and offer eternal life to those who believe. This eternal purpose will not be fulfilled until man and the earth that was cursed by Adam is restored to the sinless, pristine state that existed in the Garden of Eden. This transformation will not take place until the 1,000-year millennial kingdom has run its course, Satan and all sinners are cast down into the Lake of Fire and Brimstone (Revelation 20:10-15), and the earth has been renovated with fire (II Peter 3:10). One of the biblical truths that is generally misunderstood is that this earth will never be completely destroyed. It will be restored to the innocent and pristine state of the Garden of Eden (Revelation 21:1) and redeemed man will live here forever (Revelation 21:2-4). The saints will live forever on this new earth in a city called the New Jerusalem (Revelation 21:10); there will be no sea (Revelation 21:1); and man will once again be nourished by 12 different fruits which will grow on God's new Tree of Life (Revelation 22:1-2).

The Adamic Covenant

The Edenic Dispensation ended when Adam and Eve broke the *Edenic Covenant*, which was a *conditional* covenant between God and Adam. The result of Adam's disobedience was expulsion from the Garden of Eden, but the consequence of Adam's fall was far reaching.

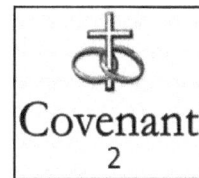
Covenant
2

Therefore, just as sin came into the world through one man, and death through sin, and so death spread to all men because all sinned.   Romans 5:12

Just as in the Edenic Covenant, the actual word *covenant* was never used when God spoke to Adam and Eve. However, recall that the word covenant means *promise*.

[13] *And the LORD God said unto the woman, What is this that thou hast done? And the woman said, The serpent beguiled me, and I did eat.*
[14] *And the LORD God said unto the serpent, Because thou hast done this, thou art cursed above all cattle, and above every beast of the field; upon thy belly shalt thou go, and dust shalt thou eat all the days of thy life:*
[15] *And I will put enmity between thee and the woman, and between thy seed and her seed; it shall bruise thy head, and thou shalt bruise his heel.*
[16] *Unto the woman he said, I will greatly multiply thy sorrow and thy conception; in sorrow thou shalt bring forth children; and thy desire shall be to thy husband, and he shall rule over thee.*
[17] *And unto Adam he said, Because thou hast hearkened unto the voice of thy wife, and hast eaten of the tree, of which I commanded thee, saying, Thou shalt not eat of it: cursed is the ground for thy sake; in sorrow shalt thou eat of it all the days of thy life;*

[18] Thorns also and thistles shall it bring forth to thee; and thou shalt eat the herb of the field;
[19] In the sweat of thy face shalt thou eat bread, till thou return unto the ground; for out of it wast thou taken: for dust thou art, and unto dust shalt thou return.
    Genesis 3:13-19

(1) Satan deceived Adam and Eve and became ruler of this world. He has deceived man ever since.

(2) The animal kingdom changed and became afraid of man. The ancient manuscript of Jubilees recorded that before the fall, the animals that lived in the Garden of Eden both lived together with and even talked with Adam and Eve.

(3) Eve was cursed along with every woman after her. She would experience pain and sorrow in childbirth (Genesis 3:16).

(4) Man was ordained to rule over woman.

(5) Food would no longer grow freely from God's trees and soil, but the ground was cursed and man would have to till and work the land to produce vegetables and fruit (man was forbidden to eat meat at that time).

(6) Thorns and thistles would grow in the fields.

(7) Animals and fowl would shun man and not live in peace with mankind.

(8) Adam was created from the dust of the earth, and upon death he would return to dust.

When God spoke to Adam and Eve, it was after they had sinned and disobeyed God. So who was really responsible for the first sin? It is common theology to place the blame upon Satan, who took the form of a serpent and tempted Eve. Certainly Satan was the *agent* of sin but one of the immutable characteristics of God is that He will always allow mankind to exercise free will: If man sins against God it is always a choice. As Christians we are constantly assailed by Satan and tempted, but the born-again Christian is able to resist Satan and his lies by calling upon God for authority and the Holy Spirit for power. But Eve was created by God and knew Him in person. We must look further if we are to place the proper blame. Surely, it must have been Eve who yielded to temptation and committed the first sin. However, if we look a little closer, it is evident that Adam was present and witnessed the whole thing when Eve fell to the Serpent's temptation.

Yes, Adam was there: Genesis 3.6 makes this clear. She took the fruit and ate, and she also gave some to her husband who was with her. The issue is not that Eve may have been deceived, but who was responsible for her behavior? The answer is at the heart of the Christian family unit today and the role that a husband must play in the family unit. Adam was right next to his wife when she was tempted. He was responsible for guarding her. He failed to intervene when his wife was being tempted, and he failed in his responsibility to safeguard the garden and his wife. Yes, Adam was responsible for disobeying God. He allowed Eve to do the one thing that God had forbidden them to do. Adam as head must take responsibility for the fall. God commissioned him to rule and subdue all creation. Ironically, a reptilian creature and a piece of fruit brought down the man who was meant to rule them. In the process he failed at protecting his wife.

The narrative of the *fall* ends where it began. Adam is the faulty responsible party. He is our federal head: *In Adam all die* (1Cor. 15.22). Adam's sin is not that he was tempted by Eve, but that he failed to lead. The woman was deceived (1Tim 2.13) but Adam allowed it by not exercising his headship, authority, and power over his wife and creation.

When Adam and Eve both sinned, it broke the conditional covenant with God and left man in a fallen state, but God would soon make a second, *unconditional* covenant with Adam and Eve (Genesis 3:14–24). Like the Edenic Covenant, the *Adamic Covenant* is not explicitly referred to as a covenant in Genesis, but it is a significant promise that God made to all mankind.

God does not tell us everything at once, but He unfolds His plan for us over time. This is called by biblical scholars, *progressive revelation.* When Adam fell he generated multiple curses upon all mankind. The alternative would have been to simply destroy Adam, Eve, and the Garden of Eden and start all over with a new plan. However, the Apostle John tells us 4,000 years later:

In the beginning was the Word, and the Word was with God, and the Word was God
John 1:1

*According to the **eternal** purpose which he purposed in Christ Jesus our Lord:*
Ephesians 3:11

Later, the writer of Hebrews revealed to us that:

[16] *For **by** him were all things created, that are in heaven, and that are in earth, visible and invisible, whether they be thrones, or dominions, or principalities, or powers: all things were created **by** him, and for him:*
[17] *And he is before all things, and **by** him all things consist.*   Colossians 1:16-17

*Thou hast put all things in subjection under his **feet**. For in that he put all in subjection under him, he left nothing that is not put under him. But now we see not yet all things put under him.* Hebrews 2:8

It is clear from these passages that God had a son and a plan since the beginning of all things. It was through His manifold wisdom and His eternal plan that the promised Messiah would be His son, Jesus Christ. The span of time and every event up until the present time were predestined by God, and the world as we know it will not come to an end until all things ordained by God have come to pass. The Edenic Dispensation and the Adamic Dispensation are both intimately tied to the fall of Adam. There is no record of anything but a set of verbal commands and promises in both dispensations. The existence of Adam and Eve upon the earth appear to be governed by the oral promises of God and the conscience of man, although as time went by the people were able to observe the actions and consequences of sin. The Adamic Dispensation, which started with the fall and ended with the great flood of Noah's day, was not guided by a formal set of written laws. Some scholars call this the *Age of Conscience*, since man's behavior was guided by his own free will and conscience, tempered by his knowledge of a Holy God. This conjecture becomes near certainty if we carefully study the incident of Cain and Abel. Adam and Eve lived in the Garden of Eden without any written laws. When they were cast out of the Garden of Eden they began to populate the earth. The first three men born to a woman were Cain (*I have gotten a man from the Lord*),

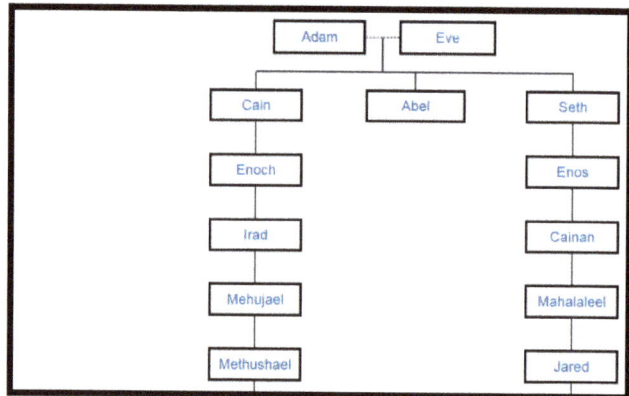

Adam		Eve	
Cain	Abel		Seth
Enoch			Enos
Irad			Cainan
Mehujael			Mahalaleel
Methushael			Jared

Abel (*breath or vanity*) and Seth (*placed or appointed*). Of course, to procreate, the sons of Adam and Eve married and were given in marriage to their sisters.

Recall that Cain and Abel offered sacrifices to the Lord, but Cain's sacrifice of fruits was not *respected* by the Lord, and Abel's sacrifice of the firstlings of his flock were accepted. Cain became jealous of his brother, Abel, and while they were both in the field, Cain slew Abel. This was the first recorded act of murder. When Cain was approached by God, he lied to Him and asked a poignant question of rebellion: *Am I my brother's keeper?* (Genesis 4:9). This question has echoed through the ages and is just as important to every Christian today as it was then. The dilemma is why did God reject the offering of

Cain? We are not told, but can only conjecture. Some have assumed that Cain was not sincere in his offering. Others have postulated that it was casual and did not require effort. Both seem out of context. It is presumed likely that at some time the Lord had made known to Cain and Abel the prophetic significance of a blood sacrifice. We may never know until we ask God himself.

Adam and Eve obviously had female children, and after a period of time in which sons and daughters married, the earth soon began to be filled with the progeny of Adam and Eve. Adam lived to the age of 930 years old, and was for some years a contemporary of Noah. Noah obviously was told firsthand about the fall of Adam, the wonders of the Garden of Eden, and the consequences of rebellion against God. The word *sin*, which means a *transgression against God,* first appears in the King James Bible in Genesis 4:7. The first recorded act of rebellion against God was when Adam and Eve disavowed the Edenic Covenant. It is formally used in relation to Cain killing his brother Abel. This, of course, prefigures the sixth of the 10 Commandments given in writing by God to Moses at Mt. Sinai.

As time passed, man became totally mired in sin and disobedience to God. The apex of their sinful nature came about when women perverted themselves by having children with a rebellious band of angels. This union produced giants in the land called *Nephilim.* Of course, this was a plan of Satan to corrupt the line of Adam which would one day produce the Christ. But the Lord was still in control of creation, and in an act of righteous anger He announced that he would flood the earth with water, killing every man and beast not under His divine protection. Finally, in Genesis 6 God issued a warning.

And the LORD said, My spirit shall not always strive with man, for that he also is flesh: yet his days shall be an hundred and twenty years.   Genesis 6:3

This verse has created some confusion. Many theologians say that man would no longer live more than 120 years, but of course this cannot be true. Noah died at age 150 years and later the patriarch Abraham lived to be 175 years old. It is more likely that this announcement was exactly as it seems to be, divine prophecy that wicked mankind was to be destroyed after 120 years had passed. The lone exception to God's promise was that Noah, his three sons and their wives would be saved in a great ark. The ark was also to save the animal kingdom from worldwide eradication.

Hence, only 1,656 years after Adam and Eve were cast out of Eden, the world and everything in it was to be covered by water, and every living thing not placed in the ark was to be destroyed. God's plan to use Adam and Eve to populate a world cursed by sin with righteous descendants of Adam and Eve had failed. It was not a failure because of God's will, but because of man's choices. God would give man another chance; He would repopulate the world with the descendants of Noah, who was a *righteous man*. This ended the *Adamic Dispensation* and gave rise to the *Noahidic Dispensation*. The covenant promises and conditions imposed upon the Noahidic Dispensation were *unconditional* and will remain in effect until the end of the ages.

The Noahidic Covenant

The Noahidic Dispensation began when Noah, his three sons, their wives and a remnant of the animal kingdom left the ark. Contrary to the previous Edenic and Adamic Dispensations, the word *covenant* is used for the first time in the Noahidic Dispensation. The covenant which God made with Noah is found in Genesis Chapter 9.

[8]*And God spoke unto Noah, and to his sons with him, saying,*
[9] *And I, behold, I establish my covenant with you, and with your seed after you;*
[10] *And with every living creature that is with you, of the fowl, of the cattle, and of every beast of the earth with you; from all that go out of the ark, to every beast of the earth.*
[11] *And I will establish my covenant with you; neither shall all flesh be cut off any more by the waters of a flood; neither shall there any more be a flood to destroy the earth.*
       Genesis 9:8-11

The covenant which God made with Noah was *unconditional; i*t was directed to Noah and all of his descendants, perpetually. God promised that He would never again destroy the world with a flood (water). However, He did not say that the world would never be destroyed again. Peter revealed to us about 2,000 years later that God would once again one day destroy the world, but this time by *fire*. This will take place following the 1,000-year Millennial Dispensation (II Peter 3:7).

It is instructive to note that in addition to the Noahidic Covenant, God set down a set of commands or laws that Noah and his descendants were commanded to follow. These Laws were known by the Jewish Rabbi's as the *Seven Noahidic Laws* (Genesis 9). These laws were to be in perpetuity, and are still in effect.

(1) Courts and judges would be set up to interpret and enforce social injustice.
(2) Blasphemy against God and taking His name in vain was a grievous sin.

(3) Idolatry and worshipping graven images was an abomination to the Lord
(4) Sexual immorality, such as incest and adultery, were strictly forbidden.
(5) Thou shalt not kill a fellow man.
(6) Thou shall not steal.
(7) No blood of an animal can be eaten.

According to the Talmud, the rabbis agree that the seven laws were given to the sons of Noah. Six of the seven laws are exegetically derived from passages in Genesis, with the seventh being the establishing of courts.

After the flood, Noah and his sons were told to *be fruitful and multiply* (Genesis 9:1). Noah and his family reproduced and began to spread north into the modern Baltic Region, and into the land surrounding the Mediterranean Sea. The Noahidic Dispensation has also been called the *Dispensation of Conscience*. This is because without any written law, the descendants of Noah did *what was in their heart*. Without a clear vision of what God requires and what He demands, the heart can become calloused, hard and rebellious. The evolution of man's thinking and actions during this period of time set a path to destruction.

At first, there was a clear vision of God and His Holiness. Then, the image of God slowly faded from their mind and inner thoughts were not focused on Godly things, but the things of this world. Man became decidedly wicked, turning to idol worship, adultery and all acts of disobedience. For the first time in recorded scripture, the importance of the blood was made clear by God.

[3] Every moving thing that liveth shall be meat for you; hereof, shall ye not eat. Even as the green herb have I given you all things.
[4] But you shall not eat flesh with its life, that is, its blood.   Genesis 9:3-4

This commandment was a shadow and type of the Levitical Sacrificial system, and was a prophetic picture of the ultimate sacrifice of Jesus Christ on the cross of Calvary.

The covenant with Noah was for all descendants of Noah, which is all mankind. God will later make a separate covenant with Abraham while he is still under the Noahidic covenant. It should be restated that the Noahidic Covenant was perpetual, and it will remain in force until the end of time.

The Abrahamic Covenant

It was certainly foreknown by God that after the great flood man would descend into the depths of rebellion and apostasy. In another act of pure love and grace, God again decided to renew a personal relationship with man. In a Land called Ur of the Chaldees, which was near where the Garden of Eden existed, there lived a man named *Terah*. Terah's father was Nahor who was a descendant of Shem. Terah worshipped idols and he was the father of Abram and Haran. Haran became the father of Lot, who was Abram's nephew.

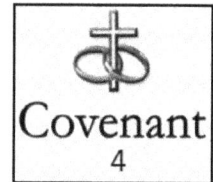

The Abrahamic covenant unfolds and develops over three distinct interactions between God and Abram. The covenant relationship between God and Abram starts in Genesis 12 and is continued through Genesis 15. Technically, the covenant with Abram is not found in Genesis 12, but in Genesis 15 where the word covenant actually appears. It is there that the specific details of the covenant are spelled out. In Chapter 12 only the general features of the covenant are introduced. God starts by commanding Abram to move to a land that God will choose (Genesis 12:1). God then promises Abram that he and his *seed* will be *blessed* when Abram responds to His call (Genesis 12:2-3). The name of Abram (later Abraham) would be great (Genesis 12:2). God would watch over and protect Abram (12:3): and a great nation will come from his loins (12:2). Finally, God tells Abram that he will be a blessing to all peoples of the earth (Genesis 12:3). To enter into these blessings Abram was only required to "go" to the land God would show him. The covenant made with Abram by God was *unconditional* and is still in effect today.

[1] Now the LORD had said unto Abram, Get thee out of thy country, and from thy kindred, and from thy father's house, unto a land that I will show thee
[2] And I will make of thee a great nation, and I will bless thee, and make thy name great; and thou shall be a blessing:
[3] And I will bless them that bless thee, and curse him that curse thee: and in thee shall all families of the earth be blessed.   Genesis 12:1-3

Later God appeared to Abram and made a *Land Covenant* with him.

[14] And the LORD said unto Abram, after that Lot was separated from him, Lift up now thine eyes, and look from the place where thou art northward, and southward, and eastward, and westward:
[15] For all the land which thou seest, to thee will I give it, and to thy seed for ever.
[16] And I will make thy seed as the dust of the earth: so that if a man can number the

dust of the earth, then shall thy seed also be numbered.
[17] Arise, walk through the land in the length of it and in the breadth of it; for I will give
it unto thee.   Genesis 13:14-17

We will see later that the land Covenant was later given again to King David. In the *Davidic Covenant*, the extent of the land was clarified and defined.

Imagine the reaction of Abram. He is married to Sarai and is living in Ur of the Chaldees. Suddenly God appears to him and tells him to leave his homeland and his kindred. He is evidently living at that time in the house of his father, Terah. What would you do if this happened to you? It must have been extremely difficult to tell his wife: *Pack up, we are leaving.* Looking surprised, she probably asks in tears: *Where are we going*? Abram responds, *I don't know yet*. She responds: *Are you drunk or just crazy*? He relates to her that *God had told him to leave. Did you see Him?* Sarai asks. *Well, no, I just heard His voice.* Abram is revered by the Jews as a man of tremendous faith, and now it should be clear that this is emphatically true. The revelation continues: Abram would ask God, *where will I go? I will lead you*, replied God. Abram asks, *Where will I live*? God replies: *I will show you, just get underway. By the way, go get Lot and his wife to go with you.*

The entire scenario is almost unbelievable, so there must have been something miraculous and awesome that caused Abram, Sarai and even his nephew Lot to load up, abandon almost everything they possessed and move south. However, Christian's today respond to much the same calling. We are commanded in the scriptures to follow Christ and bring the lost to salvation. Countless missionaries sell all they possess and respond to a foreign missionary call. The scenario is much the same, and all of this is embraced through *faith*. Like Abram, we have never seen Christ nor even spoken to Him in person; we serve Christ by faith and by faith alone.

God promised Abram five things.

     (1) He will bless Abram.
     (2) Abram's name will be great among men.
     (3) Abram will be a blessing to all mankind.
     (4) God will protect Abram; Those who bless him, God will bless; those who curse him God will curse.
     (5) I will give you land and you will prosper.

When Abram was 99 years old and Sarai was 89, God reappeared to him and reconfirmed his covenant.

[2] *And I will make my covenant between me and thee, and will multiply thee exceedingly.*
[3] *And Abram fell on his face: and God talked with him, saying,*
[4] *As for me, behold, my covenant is with thee, and thou shalt be a father of many nations.*
[5] *Neither shall thy name any more be called Abram, but thy name shall be Abraham; for a father of many nations have I made thee.*
[6] *And I will make thee exceeding fruitful, and I will make nations of thee, and kings shall come out of thee.*
[7] *And I will establish my covenant between me and thee and thy seed after thee in their generations for an everlasting covenant, to be a God unto thee, and to thy seed after thee.*
[8] *And I will give unto thee, and to thy seed after thee, the land wherein thou art a stranger, all the land of Canaan, for an everlasting possession; and I will be their God.*
[9] *And God said unto Abraham, Thou shalt keep my covenant therefore, thou, and thy seed after thee in their generations.*
[10] *This is my covenant, which ye shall keep, between me and you and thy seed after thee*   Genesis 17:2-10

God reassured Abram that he and Sarai would have a child, and He renamed Abram, *Abraham*. God then turned to Sarai and renamed her Sarah (princess).

[15] *As for Sarai thy wife, thou shalt not call her name Sarai, but Sarah shall her name be.*
[16] *And I will bless her, and give thee a son also of her: yea, I will bless her, and she shall be a mother of nations; kings of people shall be of her.*   Genesis 17: 15-16

In hearing these words, Abraham fell out laughing and said:

[17] *Shall a child be born unto him that is an hundred years old? and shall Sarah, that is ninety years old, bear?*
[18] *And Abraham said unto God, O that Ishmael might live before thee!*
                    Genesis 17:17-18

If this confrontation was not in the Holy Scriptures, it would no doubt be taken as a fictional account. Abraham actually heard God speaking and refused to believe Him! The same God who had parted the Red Sea! God could have destroyed Abraham, but He had earlier made a promise that He could not disallow. So he reassured Abraham:

And God said, Sarah thy wife shall bear thee a son indeed; and thou shalt call his name Isaac: and I will establish my covenant with him for an everlasting covenant, and with his seed after him.   Genesis 17:19

The child was to be named *Isaac* which means *he laughs* because Abraham laughed at God. Nine months later, Abraham and Sarah had the child of promise and did name him Isaac. Abraham was 100 years old and Sarah was 90.

One of the blessings Jacob received from Isaac was that other nations would bow down to the sons that would descend from Jacob (Genesis 27:29). Clearly, for this prophecy to be fulfilled, Jacob's descendants would have to become great nations and empires. This same blessing also promised that God would bless the nations that blessed Jacob's descendants, and would curse the nations that cursed Jacob's descendants.

God reiterated Abraham's blessings to Jacob in Genesis 28:10-15 by saying Jacob's descendants would be as numerous as the *dust of the earth* and they would eventually spread to all four corners of the world from the region of the Promised Land. Jacob's name was later changed to *Israel* (Genesis 32:28) which means *may God prevail*; and he had 12 sons who produced the *12 tribes of Israel*.

The family tree of Abraham, from which the 12 tribes of Israel sprang, is complicated. Contrary to modern Western customs, it was acceptable in ancient times to marry close family relatives including cousins and nieces. It was also common for men to have more than one wife, and even to have children with women who were not their wives (slaves or concubines). For example, Abraham's first son was the child of his wife's hand maiden; and biblical tradition even says that his wife Sarah was actually his half-sister. The twelve sons of Jacob were born from four different mothers: the two natural wives of Jacob (Leah and Rachel) and by two other women who were servants of Leah (Zipah and Bilhah). According to Rabbinic

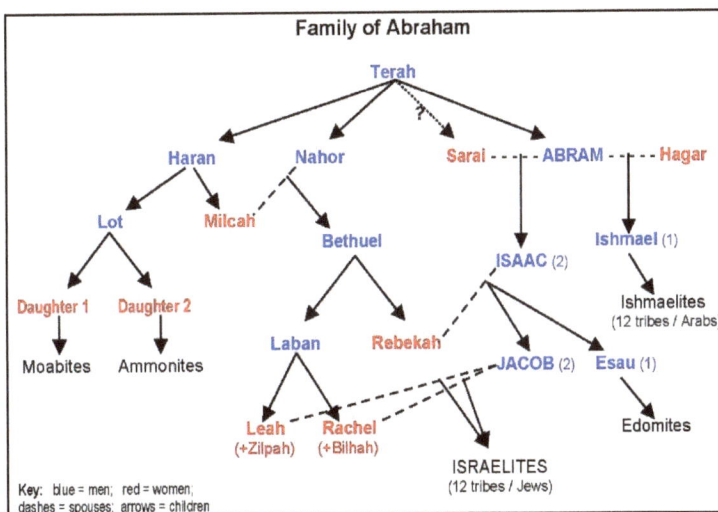
Family of Abraham

57

sources (Midrash), Zipah and Bilhah were daughters of Laban which makes them half-sisters to Leah and Rachel.

Rachel (*Joseph and Benjamin*), Bilhah (*Dan and Napthali*) and Zipah (*Gad and Asher*) each had two sons from Abraham: Leah had six sons (*Reubin, Simeon, Levi, Judah Issachar and Zebulun*). However, these are not the well-known 12 tribes of Israel. Recall that Joseph was the youngest brother, and he was the favorite son of Jacob. In jealousy, the other 11 brothers faked Joseph's death and sold him into Egyptian slavery. By divine appointment, Joseph interpreted a dream of the Pharaoh and rose to a position of authority and power, becoming the keeper of all of the grain in Egypt. Joseph had two sons: *Manasseh, and Ephraim.* He gave his birthright as one of the 12 tribes of Israel to his two sons. Simple math shows that there are now 13 tribal sons and not 12! How were the 12 tribes of Israel actually formed? The solution to this riddle would not become evident until God blessed the 13 tribes at Mt. Sinai as His chosen people. Two separate events explain this riddle. *First*, God appointed the tribe of Levi as the Royal Priesthood, and they were set apart from the other 12 tribes. *Second*, when Joshua finally conquered the Promised Land, the land was divided among the remaining 12 tribes of Israel; the Tribe of Levi received no inheritance for it was their sacred calling to *serve the people* as

The family tree of Jacob is shown below:

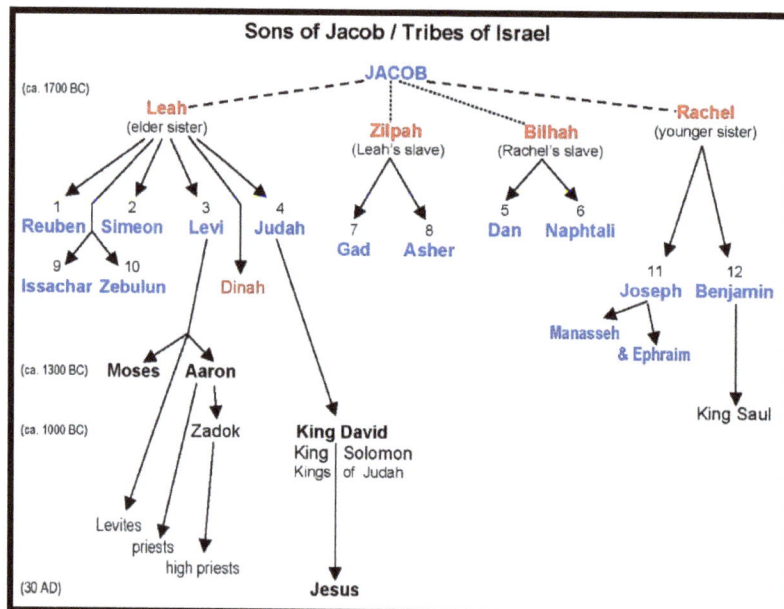

The original 12

58

tribes of Israel were all from the loins of Jacob. Joseph passed his birthright on to his two sons, Manasseh and Ephraim. Moses and Aaron were both the sons of Levi, and Jesus Christ came from the tribe of Judah. God reiterated to Jacob the covenant blessings which had been bestowed upon Abraham in Genesis 28:10-15 by saying that the descendants of Jacob would be as numerous as the *dust of the earth*, and that they would eventually spread to all four corners of the world from the region of the Land of Canaan. Jacob's name was later changed to *Israel* (Genesis 32:28), and he had 12 sons by four wives: Bilhah, Zipah, Rachel, and Leah.

It is interesting that by combining all the above points we begin to understand both the relationship and the bitter rivalries between the modern Israelites and the neighboring Semitic peoples. The Israelites (and ancient Jews) believe that the promises God made to Abraham were divinely given to them through Isaac and Jacob, while the descendants of the other tribes which eventually formed Palestine, Iraq, Iran, etc. believe that the land promised to Abraham and David also belong to them since they are descendants of the elder sons (and thus the rightful heirs) of Abraham. It is through all of this confusion that the world today is in a constant state of war, and that the nation of Israel is assailed from all sides. This is, of course, all being orchestrated by Satan. Satan knows that if he could destroy the land covenant that God made with Abraham and King David that he would disallow God's word and disrupt His eternal plans; this will never happen. It is also important to realize that any nation that blesses Israel will be blessed, and any nation that curses Israel will be cursed. It is because of this covenant promise that America has been blessed all of these years. There is currently a political movement to withdraw our alliance and support to Israel. If and when this happens, it would begin an irreversible, downward spiral of America and its greatness. Pray that this will never come to pass.

It is also interesting that the land covenant given by God to Abraham prophesied that from his loins would arise a *seed* (singular) in whom all nations would be blessed. This seed is the Messiah, Jesus Christ. The entire Jewish religion refuses to recognize this part of the Abrahamic Covenant, and will not accept that Jesus Christ is the Son of God who is their long-awaited Messiah. However, Abraham believed God and his *faith was accounted to him as righteousness*. This occurred 430 years before the Covenant of Law at Mt. Sinai. There was no written law in existence at the time of Abraham, so Abraham died in *faith* looking for the promised messiah who would take away his sins and proclaim him justified.

The offspring of Abraham prospered and grew for 215 years in the Land of Canaan. At that time, a great famine fell across all of Canaan and also over the land of Egypt. Jacob moved to Egypt because there was no water or grain in the land of Canaan. This was obviously a lack of faith on the part of Jacob, although it is not discussed or elaborated upon in scripture. It is possible that this is not mentioned by the Jewish Rabbi's because the ancient scribes did not want to taint the name of the patriarch, Jacob. However, it is also true that the movement of Jacob and either 70 or 75 people into Egypt was undoubtedly by divine intervention, and was necessary to lead to the eventual Exodus from Egypt and the giving of the Law at Mt. Sinai. God controls the affairs of man and is omniscient.

Abraham and his descendants spent 215 years in the land of Canaan and 215 years in Egypt (Galatians 3:17). Because they left the protection and promises of God and moved to Egypt, they multiplied and grew into over 2 million people, but they became slaves of Pharaoh, making bricks from mud and straw to build the magnificent temples and cities of ancient Egypt. After 215 years of living in Egypt, a man named Moses was born who would eventually deliver the nation of Israel out of bondage. Moses, at age 40, killed an Egyptian and then fled to the Land of Edom for 40 more years until God called him to free His chosen people and lead them back to the Land of Canaan. After God brought 10 plagues on Egypt, the nation of Israel was finally allowed to leave. Seventeen days later the nation of Israel crossed the Red Sea, and emerged a new holy nation under God. Forty-seven days after leaving Egypt, Moses and the people camped under the shadow of Mt. Sinai and three days later received the Law from God through His servant Moses (Phillips, Chronology). This ended the *Abrahamic Dispensation* and began the *Dispensation of the Law*. The giving of the Law at Mt. Sinai and subsequent promises by God constituted what is called the *Mosaic Covenant*, because God gave his laws and statutes for Israel to the people through Moses.

The Mosaic Covenant

God called Abram out of the Chaldees to produce a new nation that He would love and protect. God appeared to Jacob and changed his name to *Israel*. The exact meaning of Israel is disputed, but it is often defined as: *to wrestle with God, May God prevail.* This is appropriate because the chosen nation of Israel continually rebelled against God and fell away into apostasy, but God will never forsake or abandon them.

Covenant
5

The Abrahamic Covenant was unconditional, but the Mosaic Covenant was conditional and was made between God and Israel.

[5] *Now therefore, if ye will obey my voice indeed, and keep my covenant, then ye shall be a peculiar treasure unto me above all people: for all the earth is mine:*
[6] *And ye shall be unto me a kingdom of priests, and an holy nation. These are the words which thou shalt speak unto the children of Israel.*
[7] *And Moses came and called for the elders of the people, and laid before their faces all these words which the LORD commanded him.*
[8] *And all the people answered together, and said, All that the LORD hath spoken we will do. And Moses returned the words of the people unto the LORD.*   Exodus 19:5-8

The central part of the Mosaic Covenant was the giving of the Ten Commandments to Moses and the people at Mt. Sinai. However, the Jewish religion has identified a total of 613 laws that were eventually given to the Jews. God gave religious, social and dietary laws to the nation of Israel to protect them and set them apart from all other people. The Mosaic Covenant differed significantly from the Abrahamic Covenant because it was unconditional. The blessings that God promised Israel were directly related to Israel's obedience to the Mosaic Law. If Israel would be obedient, then God would bless them; if they disobeyed, then God would punish them. The blessings and curses that are associated with this conditional covenant are found in detail in Deuteronomy 28.

Most Christians today do not fully understand the significance of the Law as it stands in the *Dispensation of Grace*. It is often believed that salvation under the Law was granted to those that fulfilled the law, and that transgressions under the law were forgiven by offerings of bulls and goats at the Altar of Sacrifice in the Tabernacle, and later in the Temple. Nothing could be further from the truth. The Book of Hebrews clearly states: *For it is not possible that the blood of bulls and of goats should take away sins* (Hebrews 10:4). The Old Testament sacrificial system could never forgive sins, it simply *atoned* (covered) sins until the Messiah Jesus Christ provided a permanent and complete sacrifice for sin:

[13] *For if the blood of bulls and of goats, and the ashes of an heifer sprinkling the unclean, sanctifieth to the purifying of the flesh:*
[14] *How much more shall the blood of Christ, who through the eternal Spirit offered himself without spot to God, purge your conscience from dead works to serve the living God?*

[15] *And for this cause he is the mediator of the new testament, that by means of death, for the redemption of the transgressions that were under the first testament, they which are called might receive the promise of eternal inheritance.*   Hebrews 9:13-15

It is not that there was any problem with the Law itself, for the Law is perfect and was given by a perfect and holy God, but the Law had no power to give people new life, and the people were not able to obey the Law (Galatians 3:21). The Mosaic covenant is built upon the concept that obedience to God is necessary to receive God's divine blessings. God had already promised blessings to Israel as part of the unconditional Abrahamic Covenant, but God now initiates a new dispensation based upon the faithfulness of Israel to respond to the written laws of God.

The new Mosaic covenant was fundamentally a *works* covenant rather than a *grace* covenant. The works principle in the Mosaic Covenant is related to both blessings in this life and in the life hereafter based upon the demands of the Law. The Law was never meant to save Israel because it was impossible for anyone to fulfil all of the law. The law did not save, it brought about death in sin. The path to salvation and everlasting life had never changed nor will it ever change; salvation is by grace and faith in Jesus Christ.

The basic Mosaic Covenant is found in Exodus 19.

[3] *And Moses went up unto God, and the LORD called unto him out of the mountain, saying, Thus shalt thou say to the house of Jacob, and tell the children of Israel;*
[4] *Ye have seen what I did unto the Egyptians, and how I bare you on eagles' wings, and brought you unto myself.*
[5] *Now therefore, if ye will obey my voice indeed, and keep my covenant, then ye shall be a peculiar treasure unto me above all people: for all the earth is mine:*
[6] *And ye shall be unto me a kingdom of priests, and an holy nation. These are the words which thou shalt speak unto the children of Israel.*   Exodus 19:3-6

The nation of Israel was originally intended to be a *theocracy*. God would rule over them through Moses and those who would follow in his office. The Levitical priesthood would temporarily provide atonement for sins through a ritualistic, sacrificial system. God would speak to the people through Moses, and once a year to the high priest on the Day of Atonement in the Holy of Holies. But the people rebelled against God and his Laws and they wanted a king like every other Gentile nation. This eventually ended in disaster when the Northern Kingdom of Israel and the Southern Kingdom of Judah were both destroyed when they violated God's Covenant. God had the nation of Israel destroyed and taken into captivity because of their apostasies and sins. However, He did not completely abandon Israel because of His unconditional promises to Abraham. The nation of Israel will yet be restored to holiness during the Millennial Kingdom of 1,000 years.

The purpose of the Mosaic Covenant can be summarized in three parts. This spiritual truth is captured by (*https://www.knowingthebible.net/the-mosaic-covenant*).

First, the Law was given to reveal the righteousness and holiness of Yahweh (Ex. 19:23; Rom. 7:12; 1 Pet. 1:15) and to separate His chosen people above all other nations. (Ex. 19:6; 22:31; 31:13; Ps. 24:3-5). The chosen nation of Israel was officially given the requirements of what a Holy God expected of them. By living under the Law, they would reflect the righteousness of God. The laws of God would make them a nation chosen and set apart from all other nations (Ex. 19:5-6). If Israel lived in obedience to the Law, then they would live to a higher standard than the pagan nations (Gentiles) which surrounded them. As a result of their obedience, they would not only be refusing a pagan lifestyle, but this choice would bring greater blessings into their lives. The Gentile nations would see these blessings and want to know and also follow the God that ruled over Israel and served as their king.

Second, the law was never intended to save man, but to reveal the sinfulness of man (Matt. 5:20; Rom. 7:7-11; Gal. 3:19). As one tried to meet the requirements of the Law, they would find time after time that they could not meet the expectations of the Law. In an apparent paradox, the burden of the law would eventually be viewed as too demanding and impossible, and would tend to drive man into rebellion and idol worship. As each individual continually fell short of the requirements of the Law (Rom. 3:23), they were forced to face their own sinfulness. Hence, the sinful and rebellious nature inherited from Adam's fall brought judgment upon themselves. They knew the Law, but they would not obey the Law (Gal. 3:9-10). The principle of choice has always been available to man.

Third, the failure to observe the Law would reveal the need for a Saviour (Matt. 5:17; Rom. 8:2-4). Once one was faced with the inevitable reality that they could not live out the requirements of the Law, they realized that they needed the Messiah promised long ago to their father Abraham to forgive them of their sins. The true purpose of the law, the prophetic nature of the Levitical sacrificial system, the Feasts of Israel and the meaning of the tabernacle would be revealed in His coming (Luke 24:26-27). For those Christians who are willing to study and see the Law for what it truly represented in shadow and type, they would see Jesus. If the Jews would remove the *scales from* their eyes, they would see that Jesus Christ is their long-awaited redeemer and Messiah.

In the fullness of time Jesus Christ came and lived a perfect life under the law. Jesus said: *I have not come to abolish the law, but to fulfil every jot and tittle of the law.* Jesus Christ came and fulfilled the law for those who could not. He did what no other Jew or Gentile could do; He met the righteous expectations of the Law (Rom. 8:1-4; Gal. 3:13-14). He also took upon Himself Israel's judgment for violating the Law. Therefore, He fulfilled the Law in both its demand for righteousness and for judgment for sin. The believer is now justified and sins forgiven by the blood of Jesus, and salvation is appropriated by grace and faith. The Law was never meant to last but to point the way to grace and mercy (Jer. 31:31-34; Rom. 10:4; Gal. 3:23-26; Heb. 8:6-13). The chosen people of God were governed by the laws of God for over 1,500 years. The Dispensation of the Law would come to an end when Christ was crucified in 30 AD. During the Dispensation of the Law, God chose David as his appointed King and reiterated the land covenant that He had made to Abraham. This was called the *Davidic Covenant,* but it was not a new covenant at all but a reassurance, clarification and reiteration of the promises made to Abraham.

The Davidic Covenant

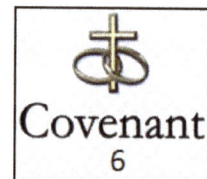

Forty-Seven years after the Mosaic Covenant was initiated at Mt. Sinai, the nation of Israel reached its highest point of achievement under King David. King David ruled as a monarch over the 12 tribes of Israel for 40 years. The military victories of King David were quite impressive and magnified his authority and the boundaries of Israel. The United Kingdom included all of the land originally allocated to the 12 tribes of Israel (except a small portion of Philistia along the southern Mediterranean coast and also the kingdom of Ammon). David eventually expanded his kingdom to the northern reaches of the Red Sea where he built an impressive fleet of ships (I Kings 9:26).

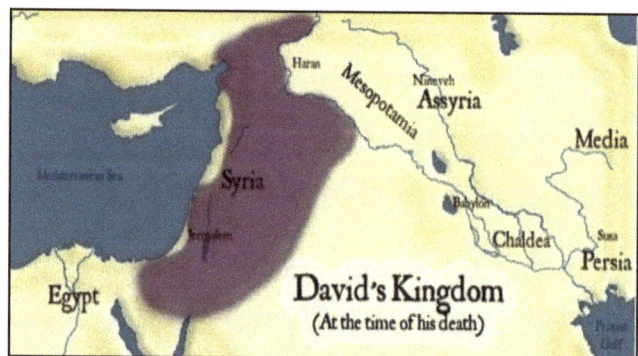

Although the United Kingdom of King David was extensive, it never encompassed the total land that had been promised to Abraham's descendants and to Moses. During the reign of King David, the Lord appeared to him and reassured him that He had not disallowed or forgotten about His covenant promise. The Davidic Covenant refers to God's promises to David through Nathan the prophet, and is found in II Samuel 7 and later summarized in I Chronicles 17:11–14 and II Chronicles 6:16. The context of this covenant was that King David lamented the fact that he was living in a magnificent palace, while the Lord was still dwelling in the Old Tabernacle built at Mt. Sinai. David inquired of Nathan the prophet as to whether or not the Lord would bless the construction of a great temple in which the Lord could visit His people. Nathan replied: *Go, do all that is in your heart; for the LORD is with you.* Later that same night, the Lord spoke to Nathan and commanded him to tell David His personal response.

[10] *I will appoint a place for my people Israel, and will plant them, that they may dwell in their own place, and be disturbed no more; and violent men shall afflict them no more, as formerly,*
[11] *from the time that I appointed judges over my people Israel; and I will give you rest from all your enemies. Moreover, the LORD declares to you that the LORD will make you a house.*
[12] *When your days are fulfilled and you lie down with your fathers, I will raise up your offspring after you, who shall come forth from your body, and I will establish his kingdom.*
[13] *He shall build a house for my name, and I will establish the throne of his kingdom forever.*
[14] *I will be his father, and he shall be my son. When he commits iniquity, I will chasten him with the rod of men, with the stripes of the sons of men;*
[15] *but I will not take my steadfast love from him, as I took it from Saul, whom I put away from before you.*
[16] *And your house and your kingdom shall be made sure for ever before me; your throne shall be established forever.*
                    II Samuel 7: 10-16

The response which God gave to King David is known as the *Davidic Covenant*, or the *Land Covenant*. We prefer the Davidic Covenant because His response is much broader and sweeping than land. Theologians are divided as to whether or not this was a real covenant, because the word never appears in the Lord's response to Nathan. However, David certainly thought that this was a Holy Covenant. David later wrote in Psalms 89:

[3] *I (God) have made a covenant with my chosen one, I have sworn to David my servant:*
[4] *I will establish your descendants forever ,and build your throne for all generations.*
                    Psalms 89:3-4

The provisions of the Davidic covenant include the following:

(1) David is to have a child, yet to be born, who shall succeed him and establish his kingdom.
(2) This son (Solomon) shall build the temple instead of David.
(3) The throne of his kingdom shall be established forever.
(4) The throne will not be taken away from him (Solomon) even though his sins justify otherwise.
(5) David's house, throne, and kingdom shall be established forever.

The New Covenant

The Dispensation of the Law lasted over 1,500 years. This dispensation was coming to a close when Jesus Christ of Nazareth came to the Jordan River to be baptized into His earthly ministry by John the Baptist. As John was preaching and baptizing the people to repentance, he looked down a dusty road and announced the arrival of the Son of God. John said: *Behold the Lamb of God who taketh away the sins of the world.* The typical Christian today would simply recognize this statement as a poetic announcement, but to the Jews of 26 AD this announcement was both prophetic and astounding. God had long ago prophesied to Adam, Abraham, David and all of the Old Testament prophets of a Messiah that would arise and take away the sins of the people. In the Dispensation of the Law, the Levitical priesthood stood before the Altar of Sacrifice killing lambs for the atonement of sins. However, every Jew understood that this was only a *covering* for sin until the type is fulfilled by the antitype. The writer of the book of Hebrews made this clear when it was written that *The blood of bulls and goats cold never take away sin.* The only permanent forgiveness of sin would not be realized until Jesus Christ, the only Son of God and the perfect sacrificial Lamb, was slain on the cross of Calvary and accepted by God. Hence, every Jew should have been rejoicing when John made his declaration. Instead, for the next 3.5 years the Jewish religious leaders sought to discredit and remove the Son of God from their society. In a perfect act of irony, the sacrificial death of Jesus Christ on the cross of Calvary both took away the sins of the whole world, and satisfied the rebellious Jews. The failure of the Jews to corporately accept Jesus Christ as their long-awaited Messiah will continue until the second coming of Christ, at which time they will finally accept Him as their redeemer. After Israel is spiritually restored, Christ will establish His millennial kingdom on earth. The salvation of Israel will involve both a spiritual awakening and a geographical home: *I will put my Spirit in you and you will live, and I*

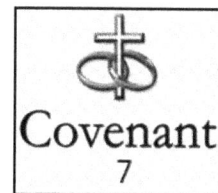

66

will settle you in your own land (Ezekiel 37:14). When Christ died on the cross of Calvary, the Law given at Mt. Sinai, which was written on stone, would from that point on be written upon the heart. Salvation so eagerly awaited by all mankind from Adam to the cross would be offered freely by grace, and not by works *lest any man should boast.*

The *New Covenant* began at the cross of Calvary when Christ cried out *It is finished.* Condemnation under the Law was finished; the Levitical sacrificial system was finished; and waiting for the long-awaited Jewish Messiah was finished. But this was not all. When Christ arose from the grave after three days and three nights, the curse of death was finished. The resurrection of Christ, the Firstfruit of all who would believe upon His holy name, was our guarantee and deposit of the resurrection from the grave for all who would believe and follow after Him. For those who died believing in Jesus Christ, this great event will happen at the *last trump* in what we now call the *Rapture* of all true believers following the end of the Great Tribulation Period described by the Apostle John in the Book of Revelation. The Rapture of the Church, which will shortly be followed by the Great Battle of Armageddon, will end the Age of Grace. This dispensation has now been going on for almost 2,000 years and will end when God says it will end.

Following the resurrection from the grave and the ascension of Jesus Christ to His Father in heaven, Christ commanded His disciples to go to Jerusalem and wait for him to join them there 47 days later. The astute reader will immediately recognize that the appearance of Jesus Christ to His disciples who were waiting in the upper room *exactly* corresponded to the Feast of Pentecost which was ordained by God at Mt. Sinai to commemorate the giving of the 10 commandments. The disciples were gathered in Jerusalem in the upper room to receive from Christ *the promise of the Father*. The promise was that Jesus Christ was no longer in the grave and would never leave them, and this promise was ratified by the giving of the Holy Spirit to all born-again believers. The disciples were joined together with other true believers, 120 in all, as the Holy Spirit fell upon them in *tongues of fire.* This was on the day of the Feast of Pentecost, and Jerusalem was filled with Jews from every country and city throughout the known world. The *sign* of the Holy Spirit was manifested by the disciples speaking in *tongues*. This was not the unintelligible, mysterious heavenly language taught by Pentecostals, but the utterance of the gospel message in every language which was spoken by the thousands of Jews who had gathered in Jerusalem. The real meaning of this event has done more to confuse believers than any other one thing in the New Testament.

The saving grace of the Gospel message went out from that day throughout the known world. The Apostle Paul, after he was converted on the Road to Damascus, was sent to the *Gentiles* while the Apostle Peter was sent primarily to *Messianic Jews*. The other disciples were sent throughout the world. All would be martyred and meet a violent death except the Apostle John, who simply disappeared around the age of 90 years old while he was at Ephesus.

The work of each disciple gave rise to the *Apostolic Age,* in which men and women of faith continued the spread of Christianity. The Catholic Church emerged in Rome and Christianity began to grow all over the world. The Christian religion grew and flourished until Constantine joined the church to the state and became the sovereign ruler of both. Of course, God never intended that the church would be married to a ruler or a king. In the Old Testament it was strictly forbidden for any King of Israel to serve as a high priest. However, the building up of the house of God always required the priesthood and the kingship to coexist. When the tabernacle was constructed, Moses represented the kingship, and Aaron represented the priesthood. When Solomon's temple was built, Solomon represented the kingship, and the high priest represented the priesthood *(Living Stream Ministry)*. The mixing of a ruler's authority with God's chosen priesthood was always a serious violation of God's plan. Recall that King Uzziah offered incense before the Lord in the temple which was a duty strictly given to the Levitical priesthood. In His righteous anger, God smote King Uzziah with leprosy which afflicted him all the remaining days of his life.

The *Battle of the Milvian Bridge* took place between the Roman Emperors Constantine I and Maxentius on October 28, 312. Constantine had a vast army at his disposal, but he believed that he needed divine help. He sought help from the Hebrew God YAHWEH, and after praying he saw the sign of a cross of light in the heavens, above the sun, and bearing the inscription: *By this symbol you will conquer*. He was successful in the ensuing battle, converted to Christianity, and declared Christianity to become the official religion of the Roman Empire. He banned crucifixion and treated the Jews with much respect. In 313 AD in the Edict of Milan, Constantine announced "that it was proper that the Christians and all others should have liberty to follow that mode of religion which to each of them appeared best", thereby granting tolerance to all religions, including Christianity. This edict also made

the empire officially neutral with regard to religious worship. Constantine made Christianity legal and ended any remaining persecution of it, but he did not go any further than that. Apart from ceasing any state sponsorship of paganism and putting some restrictions on public sacrifice, he did not limit the practice of pagan rites in any way. *Theodosius* came to power 42 years after the death of Constantine. By that time, Christianity was by far the most popular religion in the Empire and paganism was dying out. On February 27, 380 AD he passed the edict of *Cunctos populos*, also known as the *Edict of Thessalonica*, which declared that Trinitarian Christianity as defined by the Nicene Creed was the only legitimate religion in the Roman Empire. He declared followers of other forms of Christianity to be *foolish madmen*. However, after the union of church and state by Theodosius, the religious growth of Christianity gained in number by edict, but declined in spiritual blessings and holiness. When the Roman Empire went into decline, it was followed a 1,000-year period of what was called the *dark ages* (500 AD-1500 AD).

In the 16th century AD, a religious resurrection took place called the *reformation*. The most important figure of the 16th century reformation was a theologian called *Martin Luther*. Luther rejected many of the practices and beliefs of the Medieval Catholic Church, and in 1517 AD he published his ninety-five-page thesis of doctrine. Luther taught that salvation and subsequent eternal life is not earned by good deeds but is received only as a free gift of God's grace through faith in Jesus Christ. The theology of Martin Luther challenged the authority and office of both the Pope and the Catholic Church by teaching that the Bible is the only source of divinely-revealed knowledge from God, and that salvation is by faith and grace alone, not by works. Luther was condemned by the Catholic Church and was labeled a heretic for the rest of his life. However, his doctrine produced the *Protestant Reformation* from which sprang many modern religious denominations and the evangelical movement.

The *church age* began on the Day of Pentecost in 30 AD, in which all born-again Christians were indwelled with the Holy Spirit. Regardless of religious affiliation, the *Body of Christ* is composed of all believers, living and dead. This body of Christ is called the *ecclesia*, or the *called out ones*. Salvation is granted by grace during this dispensation and is by faith in Jesus Christ.

The body of Christ has been growing since 30 AD, and will continue to grow until Christ returns at His second advent. The next major event in this current age will be the rise of a prophesied man-beast called the *Antichrist*. The antichrist will be controlled and empowered by Satan, and together with the *False Prophet* he will bring about unprecedented worldwide persecution and destruction upon all Christians and Jews. The Antichrist will rule the world for 3.5 years; The Nazi holocaust which killed millions of Jews will seem like a walk in the park compared to the suffering and affliction which will take place during the tribulation period (Phillips; *The Book of Revelation: Mysteries Revealed*).

The Age of Grace will come to an end when Jesus Christ returns to earth at His second advent and fights the Battle of Armageddon outside of Jerusalem. It is widely believed that the battle of Armageddon will take place on the plain of Megiddo, some sixty miles north of Jerusalem. More than two hundred battles have been fought in that region. The plain of Megiddo and the nearby plain of Esdraelon will likely be the focal point for the battle of Armageddon. Satan and all of his followers will be completely destroyed; both the beast called the Antichrist and the False Prophet will be cast alive into the Lake of Fire; and Satan will be bound and cast into the Bottomless pit for 1,000 years. This period of 1,000 years is called the *Millennial Kingdom.* The 1,000-year Millennial Kingdom is identical to the *Millennial Dispensation*

The Millennial Covenant

The *Millennial Covenant* is not specifically called out in the biblical records, nor does the word *Millennial* which means 1,000 in Latin. Recall that the word covenant means *promises.*

Covenant
8

The term Millennial Kingdom has been adopted by theologians and prophecy teachers to stand for the 1,000 year-period during which the Children of Israel will finally fulfill the land covenant given to Abram and King David. The 1,000-year period following the Dispensation of Grace is prophesied many times in both the Old and New Testaments.

We are indebted to John F. Walvoord for the following commentary:

> *Scripture speaks of kingdoms in various forms, sometimes kingdoms relating to this world and sometimes spiritual kingdoms where God is recognized as the ruler. The Millennial Kingdom is primarily a political kingdom, though it has spiritual aspects and Jesus Christ is the King of Kings, who has come to reign over the earth. Because it is an earthly kingdom with Christ on the throne, it obviously cannot be fulfilled in the present age when Christ is in heaven.*

Jesus Christ will serve as King of Kings and Lord of Lords in the Millennial Kingdom and will fulfill the promises that He will sit on the throne of David ruling over the House of Israel (2 Sam. 7:16; Ps. 89:20-37; Isa. 11:1-16; Jer. 33:19-21). In His relationship to Israel as her king, He was born to rule over her (Luke 1:32-33). The people of Israel rejected Him as their king when He walked upon the earth, (Mark 15:12-13; Luke 19:14). Christ died as the prophesied suffering servant*: He will come again as the King of Kings who will fulfill prophecies of His ruling over the Davidic kingdom (Rev. 19:16).*

Christ will rule and reign over the entire world (Isa. 2:1-4; 9:6-7; 11:1-10; 16:5; 24:23; 32:1; 40:1-11; 42:3-4; 52:7-15; 55:4; Dan. 2:44; 7:27; Micah 4:1-8; 5:2-5; Zech. 9:9; 14:16-17). These verses demand a literal kingdom and a literal reign of Christ on earth. When Christ will reign over the people of Israel, David will be resurrected as king and serve as a co-regent under Christ (Jer. 30:9; 33:15-17; Ezek. 34:23-24; 37:24-25; Hosea 3:5). The Millennial Kingdom will be an absolute rule of Christ, and it will involve judgment on any who reject Him *(Ps. 2:9; 72:9-11; Isa. 11:4).*   John F. Walvoord, https://bible.org/seriespage/15-second-coming-christ-and-millennial-kingdom

The covenant promises of the Millennial Dispensation will be in effect for 1,000 years. During this period of time, Christ will rule over all of the earth, assisted by the body of Christ who will serve as Kings and priests (Revelation 1:6). The Millennial Kingdom will be a magnificent period of time.

- The wolf will lie with the lamb, and the leopard shall lie down with the kid; and the calf and the young lion and the fatling together; and a little child shall lead them. (Isaiah 11:6)
- God will be their theocratic dictator, and Christ will reign on the earth, sitting upon the throne of David. (Luke 1: 32-33)
- The Land promised to Israel in the Abrahamic Covenant will be inherited by the people of Israel who have turned to Jesus Christ as their Messiah: They will live in the promised land for 1,000 years.
- As the Millennial Kingdom begins, *all* of Israel will be gathered from the four corners of the earth and judged. This is called the judgment of the *Sheep and Goat* nations (Matthew 25: 32-33). This event is almost universally confused with the birth of the nation of Israel which occurred in 1948. False teachings herald the rise of Israel as a recognized nation as

71

the long-awaited return of the people of Israel to the Promised Land, but this is not biblically correct. It is true that many Jews are now returning to live in Israel, but this is *not* the return prophesied repeatedly in the Old Testament. In fact, the Jewish Nation has never reclaimed the land of Palestine or the Temple Mount from foreign occupation. These events will not happen until the Millennial Kingdom is established by Jesus Christ.

- The lifespan of man will be considerably increased, but there will still be death. (Isaiah 65: 20-25)
- Satan will be bound and cast into the bottomless pit for 1,000 years (Revelation 20:2), but the curse of Adam will cause people to sin and rebel against God. (Revelation 20:7-8)

Some scholars call this the *Age of Perfection* but it will be far from perfect. In fact, even without Satan in the world, man will ultimately rebel against God and will fall into apostasy. The nations during the Millennial Kingdom will be required to observe the Feast of Tabernacles every year in Jerusalem. Those who fail to do so will be punished by no rain (Zachariah 14:17). At the end of this 1,000-year period, Satan will be released for a *short while*. He will once again gather all unbelievers from all the world to fight against God. However, all unbelievers and those who follow after Satan will once again be completely destroyed and Satan will be cast forever into the Lake of Burning Fire (Revelation 20:7-9). Once the earth is purged of all unbelievers, all who have died during the Millennial Kingdom, all who remain alive and all unbelievers from Adam to that point in time will be brought before God for the *Great White Throne* Judgment. Only those true believers who have accepted Jesus Christ during the Millennial Kingdom will remain in God's presence; the world will be completely consumed by fire to redeem the earth which had been cursed when Adam and Eve sinned; eternity will begin. This will bring to a close the *Seven Dispositions of this Earth.*

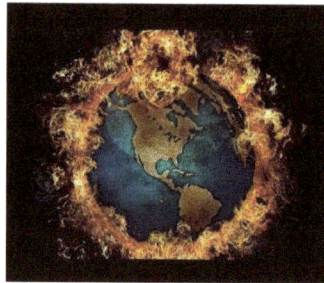

Part V: Signs and Wonders

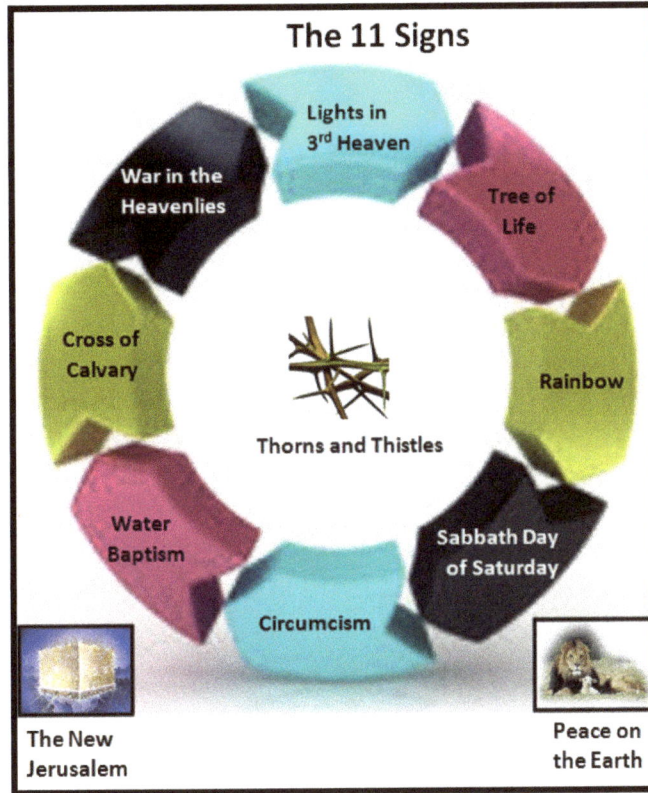

The 11 Signs

Lights in 3rd Heaven

Tree of Life

War in the Heavenlies

Cross of Calvary

Rainbow

Thorns and Thistles

Water Baptism

Sabbath Day of Saturday

Circumcism

The New Jerusalem

Peace on the Earth

During the 7 Dispensations of time the Lord has given us or will give us 11 different visible signs that His word is everlasting and His actions are just. These signs are given to remind man that God is faithful and true.

Lights in the Heavenly Realm

God created the heavens and the earth (Genesis 1:1). *And God said, Let there be lights in the firmament of the heaven to divide the day from the night; and let them be for **signs**, and for seasons, and for days, and years* (Genesis 1:14). *The heavens declare his righteousness, and all the people see his glory* (Psalms 97:6). God gave stars in the heaven as *a sign* of His creative work.

Tree of Knowledge of Good and Evil

When God created Adam and Eve, He place them in the garden and gave them dominion over all the animals. He also permitted them to roam freely about the Garden of Eden and to eat the fruit of every tree that grew there, except one, The Tree of the Knowledge of Good and Evil. Although never designated as a *sign* I believe that it could be properly recognized as such. It stood in the midst of the Garden and was undoubtedly recognized as different from everything else. Adam and Eve could look at and probably even touch the great tree, but they could not partake of its fruit. Ask any casual Christian what they would recall about the Garden of Eden, and they will likely say the Tree of the Knowledge of Good and Evil. In type, we will consider it a sign of the covenant relationship between YAWEH and man.

After Adam and Eve fell, they were expelled from the Garden of Eden and forced to toil and labor for their food. They were not allowed to eat meat, so their entire existence came from the cursed land. Anyone who has planted a garden and sowed seed knows that there is one enemy which constantly fights against a good crop; that enemy is weeds and thorns.

[17] *And unto Adam he said, Because thou hast hearkened unto the voice of thy wife, and hast eaten of the tree, of which I commanded thee, saying, Thou shalt not eat of it: cursed is the ground for thy sake; in sorrow shalt thou eat of it all the days of thy life;*
[18] *Thorns also and thistles shall it bring forth to thee; and thou shalt eat the herb of the field;*
[19] *In the sweat of thy face shalt thou eat bread, till thou return unto the ground; for out of it wast thou taken: for dust thou art, and unto dust shalt thou return.*   Genesis 3:17-19

Thorns and Thistles

Although there was no sign designated in the scriptures for the Adamic Covenant, it seems appropriate to designate thorns and thistles as a sign that the blissful and casual life for Adam and Eve was finished.

[23] *Therefore the LORD God sent him forth from the garden of Eden, to till the ground from whence he was taken.*

[24] So he drove out the man; and he placed at the east of the garden of Eden Cherubims, and a flaming sword which turned every way, to keep the way of the tree of life Genesis 3: 23-24

Note that when God decreed that the ground was cursed, this was an everlasting and unconditional action. Any farmer today is reminded of the penalty that Adam and Eve had to pay for disobeying and rebelling against God.

When the earth became corrupted and deceitful God decreed that the world would be covered with water by a great flood, and every living animal, man and woman would be destroyed except for those saved in Noah's Ark.

[7] And the LORD said, I will destroy man whom I have created from the face of the earth; both man, and beast, and the creeping thing, and the fowls of the air; for it repenteth me that I have made them.
[8] But Noah found grace in the eyes of the LORD. Genesis 6:7-8

[12] And God looked upon the earth, and, behold, it was corrupt; for all flesh had corrupted his way upon the earth.
[13] And God said unto Noah, The end of all flesh is come before me; for the earth is filled with violence through them; and, behold, I will destroy them with the earth.
Genesis 6:12-13

[19] And the waters prevailed exceedingly upon the earth; and all the high hills, that were under the whole heaven, were covered.
[20] Fifteen cubits upward did the waters prevail; and the mountains were covered.
[21] And all flesh died that moved upon the earth, both of fowl, and of cattle, and of beast, and of every creeping thing that creepeth upon the earth, and every man:
[22] All in whose nostrils was the breath of life, of all that was in the dry land, died.
Genesis 6:19-22

The Rainbow

After the flood, God gave Adam a sign in the sky that He would never again purge the world with water.

[8] And God spake unto Noah, and to his sons with him, saying,
[9] And I, behold, I establish my covenant with you, and with your seed after you;

[10] And with every living creature that is with you, of the fowl, of the cattle, and of every beast of the earth with you; from all that go out of the ark, to every beast of the earth.
[11] And I will establish my covenant with you; neither shall all flesh be cut off any more by the waters of a flood; neither shall there anymore be a flood to destroy the earth.
[12] And God said, This is the token of the covenant which I make between me and you and every living creature that is with you, for perpetual generations:
[13] I do set my bow in the cloud, and it shall be for a token of a covenant between me and the earth. Genesis 9:8-13

This sign was also unconditional, and it can still be seen in the sky today after a rainstorm.

Circumcism

God saw that the earth had become wicked and in a pure act of love and grace he called forth Abram out of the Ur of Chaldee to go to a land called Canaan. God prophesied to Abram that he would have a son of promise from which the world would be populated with His chosen people which He called Israel. This was when Abram was 76 years old and his wife Sari was 67 years old.

After 10 more years, Sari had not yet conceived, and she decided to take matters into her own hands to fulfill the covenant that God had made with Abram to *birth many nations out of his loins* by giving her handmaiden, *Hagar* to lay with him and conceive. They had a male child and named him *Ishmael*. This was not the child that God had promised to Abram, but one born out of failure to trust and believe God's word. God spoke to Abram, changed his name to Abraham, and made with him a threefold, *unconditional* covenant.

[1] And when Abram was ninety years old and nine, the LORD appeared to Abram, and said unto him, I am the Almighty God; walk before me, and be thou perfect.
[2] And I will make my covenant between me and thee, and will multiply thee exceedingly.
[3] And Abram fell on his face: and God talked with him, saying,
[4] As for me, behold, my covenant is with thee, and thou shalt be a father of many nations.
[5] Neither shall thy name any more be called Abram, but thy name shall be Abraham; for a father of many nations have I made thee.
[6] And I will make thee exceeding fruitful, and I will make nations of thee, and kings shall come out of thee.
[7] And I will establish my covenant between me and thee and thy seed after thee in their

76

generations for an everlasting covenant, to be a God unto thee, and to thy seed after thee. [8] And I will give unto thee, and to thy seed after thee, the land wherein thou art a stranger, all the land of Canaan, for an everlasting possession; and I will be their God. [9] And God said unto Abraham, Thou shalt keep my covenant therefore, thou, and thy seed after thee in their generations.

[10] This is my covenant, which ye shall keep, between me and you and thy seed after thee; Every man child among you shall be circumcised. Genesis 17:1-10

The *sign* of this covenant was that every male in Israel should be *circumcised* to confirm the covenant that God had made with Abram and all of his descendants. God *cut* this covenant with Abram by having Abram slaughter innocent animals, cut them in half, arrange their severed carcasses in a long straight line, sprinkling their blood on the ground between the carcasses and then walking between them as Abram slept in a deep sleep. This was a unilateral covenant that God appropriated to Abram by swearing to Himself; there was no other higher power to satisfy. God then changed the name of *Abram* to *Abraham*.

Circumcision served as a permanent (and painful) reminder to Israel that they needed to obey God's laws, but circumcision was not a guarantee that any Israelite would keep the commands of God or the demands of the law which would be put into place 430 years later. This was made clear by the Apostle Paul.

For circumcision is indeed profitable if you keep the law; but if you are a breaker of the law, your circumcision has become uncircumcision. Romans 2:25

The scriptures record that Abram was renamed Abraham, and both he and Ishmael were circumcised to ratify the covenant promises. One year later when Abraham was 100 years old and Sarah was 90 years, Isaac was born.

The physical act of circumcision was not nearly as important as the actual obedience that would be required of Israel when the Law came at Mt. Sinai.

[26] Therefore if the uncircumcision keep the righteousness of the law, shall not his uncircumcision be counted for circumcision?
[27] And shall not uncircumcision which is by nature, if it fulfil the law, judge thee, who by the letter and circumcision dost transgress the law?
[28] For he is not a Jew, which is one outwardly; neither is that circumcision, which is outward in the flesh:

[29] *But he is a Jew, which is one inwardly; and circumcision is that of the heart, in the spirit, and not in the letter; whose praise is not of men, but of God*   Romans 2:26-29

Every Christian today is living under the New Covenant in the Age of Grace. Having discussed the covenant sign of circumcision in its Old Testament under the Law of Moses, we now need to consider its New Testament counterpart. Paul described circumcision under the law as *a seal of the righteousness of faith.*

He (Abraham) received the sign of circumcision, a seal of the righteousness of the faith which he had while uncircumcised, that he might be the father of all who believe without being circumcised, that righteousness might be reckoned to them.   Romans. 4:11

The main argument in Romans 4 is that Abraham was justified by faith *before* he had been circumcised. This same faith was what would save all from the creation of Adam to the end of time. Abraham was called the *father* of all those of faith both before and after him. Abraham was the father of every Israelite *before* the law and *after* the law was given. This is the same faith that saves every person from the day that Christ was crucified to the current point in time. When God made his covenant with Abraham, He instituted a sign to every Child of Israel that would not only believe in Him, but in the promised Messiah (Jesus Christ) who would arise and provide permanent forgiveness of sins forever. The ritual of circumcism is still practiced today by all Jews. Circumcism is also practiced among the majority of Christians today, but not for the same reason as by the Jewish religion. There is some evidence that circumcision has multiple health benefits, including: A decreased risk of urinary tract infections, a reduced risk of some sexually transmitted diseases in men, protection against penile cancer and a reduced risk of cervical cancer in female sex partners.

The Sabbath Day

Just as before the great flood, the nation of Israel grew in number but miserably failed God and chose to disobey Him. The result was 215 years of slavery in the Land of Egypt. But God is gracious and longsuffering. and He heard the cries of the people.

[6] *Moreover he said, I am the God of thy father, the God of Abraham, the God of Isaac, and the God of Jacob. And Moses hid his face; for he was afraid to look upon God.*
[7] *And the LORD said, I have surely seen the affliction of my people which are in Egypt, and have heard their cry by reason of their taskmasters; for I know their sorrows;*
[8] *And I am come down to deliver them out of the hand of the Egyptians, and to bring*

them up out of that land unto a good land and a large, unto a land flowing with milk and honey; unto the place of the Canaanites, and the Hittites, and the Amorites, and the Perizzites, and the Hivites, and the Jebusites.

[9] *Now therefore, behold, the cry of the children of Israel is come unto me: and I have also seen the oppression wherewith the Egyptians oppress them.*

[10] *Come now therefore, and I will send thee unto Pharaoh, that thou mayest bring forth my people the children of Israel out of Egypt.*   Exodus 3:6-10

So God rescued His people from Egyptian slavery using Moses, His servant. After the great miracle at the Red Sea where God destroyed the Pharaoh and all of his forces, He led them to Mt. Sinai where once again He drew the people to Him and set them apart.

[4] *Ye have seen what I did unto the Egyptians, and how I bare you on eagles' wings, and brought you unto myself.*

[5] *Now therefore, if ye will obey my voice indeed, and keep my covenant, then ye shall be a peculiar treasure unto me above all people: for all the earth is mine:*

[6] *And ye shall be unto me a kingdom of priests, and an holy nation. These are the words which thou shalt speak unto the children of Israel.*   Exodus 19:4-6

When the Lord spoke to Moses on Mt. Sinai, He gave Moses a sign which would signify His promises

[12] *And the LORD spake unto Moses, saying,*

[13] *Speak thou also unto the children of Israel, saying, Verily my sabbaths ye shall keep: for it is a sign between me and you throughout your generations; that ye may know that I am the LORD that doth sanctify you.*

[14] *Ye shall keep the sabbath therefore; for it is holy unto you: every one that defileth it shall surely be put to death: for whosoever doeth any work therein, that soul shall be cut off from among his people.*

[15] *Six days may work be done; but in the seventh is the sabbath of rest, holy to the LORD: whosoever doeth any work in the sabbath day, he shall surely be put to death.*

[16] *Wherefore the children of Israel shall keep the sabbath, to observe the sabbath throughout their generations, for a perpetual covenant.*

[17] *It is a sign between me and the children of Israel for ever: for in six days the LORD made heaven and earth, and on the seventh day he rested, and was refreshed.*
        Exodus 31:12-17

At Mt. Sinai when God gave the Law to Moses and the Children of Israel He commanded them to observe the Sabbath day as a sign of their covenant relationship. The Sabbath day in this sign was Saturday and not Sunday. So how did Sunday eventually come to be the New Testament Sabbath day? Are we violating God's commands?

There is much confusion today among New Testament Christians concerning whether church services should be held on Saturday or Sunday. The issue revolves around the scriptures in Exodus 31: 3-17 and the creation account in Exodus1-3. First, we should note again that the seventh day in this record is Saturday and not Sunday. Saturday was always designated as the seventh day since time began. Second, we note that the primary directive was to: (1) Keep the Sabbath Holy, and (2) To observe the Sabbath as a day of rest. Third, the Sabbath was to be a perpetual observance. Note carefully that the Sabbath day was a *sign between Israel and God.* The Sabbath day of Saturday, regarded as the seventh day of creation, has always been observed by the Jews from when the law was given at Mt. Sinai in 1450 until today.

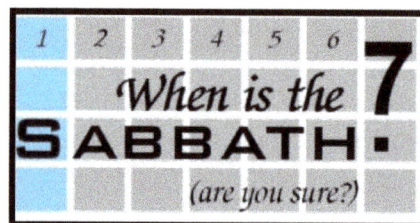

In both Old and New Testament there is not a shadow of variation in the doctrine of the Sabbath. The seventh day, Saturday, is the only day ever designated by the term Sabbath in the entire Bible. Not only was Jesus a perfect example in observing the weekly seventh-day Sabbath, but all His disciples followed the same pattern after Jesus had gone back to heaven. Yet no intimation of any change of the day is made. The apostle Paul, who wrote pages of counsel about lesser issues of Jewish and Gentile conflicts, had not one word to say about any controversy over the day of worship. Circumcision, foods offered to idols, and other Jewish customs were readily challenged by early Gentile Christians in the church, but the weightier matter of weekly worship never was an issue. Why? For the simple reason that no change was made from the historic seventh day of Old Testament times, and from creation itself. Had there been a switch from the Sabbath to the first day of the week, you can be sure the controversy would have been more explosive than any other to those Jewish Christians. http://www.sabbathtruth.com/sabbath-history/how-the-sabbath-was-changed

The observance of the seventh day (Saturday) as the Sabbath Day was honored by all the disciples and by Jesus himself. The observance of the Sabbath Day on the first day of the week (Sunday) was by the edict of the Roman Catholic Church. The Catholic Church maintains that it changed the Sabbath from Saturday to Sunday to honor Jesus Christ, who arose from the grave on a Sunday. From the Convert's Catechism of Catholic Doctrine by Reverend Peter Giermann: ***Question***: Which is the Sabbath day? ***Answer***: Saturday is the Sabbath day. ***Question***: Why do we observe Sunday instead of Saturday? ***Answer***: We observe Sunday instead of Saturday because the Catholic Church in the Council of Laodicea transferred the solemnity from Saturday to Sunday." That change was made about fifteen centuries before Protestantism was born, and by that time the custom was universally observed. However, the Encyclopedia Britannica under the article, *Sunday* asserts that: *It was Constantine who first made a law for the proper observance of Sunday and who appointed that it should be regularly celebrated throughout the Roman empire.* To resolve this issue, it is likely that the Roman Catholic Church did indeed change the Sabbath day from Saturday to Sunday, and after his conversion Constantine passed a law requiring all Romans to celebrate the Sabbath on a Sunday. Many churches have continued this new custom even though it rests upon the authority of the Catholic Church and not upon an explicit text from the Bible.

The crux of the matter is to fully understand what the Sabbath Day means to a New Covenant believer. We quote verbatim from the website *gotquestions.org* who we believe has accurately and scripturally addressed this issue.

> *Scripture never mentions any Sabbath (Saturday) gatherings by believers for fellowship or worship. However, there are clear passages that mention the first day of the week. For instance, Acts 20:7 states that "on the first day of the week we came together to break bread." In 1 Corinthians 16:2 Paul urges the Corinthian believers "on the first day of every week, each one of you should set aside a sum of money in keeping with his income." Since Paul designates this offering as "service" in 2 Corinthians 9:12, this collection must have been linked with the Sunday worship service of the Christian assembly. Historically Sunday, not Saturday, was the normal meeting day for Christians in the church, and its practice dates back to the first century.*

> *The Sabbath was given to Israel, not the church. The Sabbath is still Saturday, not Sunday, and has never been changed. But the Sabbath is part of the Old Testament Law, and Christians are free from the bondage of the Law (Galatians 4:1-26; Romans 6:14). Sabbath keeping is not required of the Christian, be it Saturday or Sunday. The first day of the week, Sunday, the Lord's Day*

(Revelation 1:10) celebrates the New Creation, with Christ as our resurrected Head. We are not obligated to follow the Mosaic Sabbath resting, but are now free to follow the risen Christ, serving. The Apostle Paul said that each individual Christian should decide whether to observe a Sabbath rest, "One man considers one day more sacred than another; another man considers every day alike. Each one should be fully convinced in his own mind" (Romans 14:5). We are to worship God every day, not just on Saturday or Sunday.

Sunday was chosen because on that day was wrought the greatest miracle of the Christian religion, the resurrection of Christ from the dead. It was on Sunday also that the Holy Ghost descended upon the Apostles and sent them out to preach the Gospel to the world. Sunday is, therefore, the birthday of the Christian church.

Authors note: The Sabbath day was observed every Saturday by both the apostles and Christ during His earthly ministry. the first day of the month was also set aside to worship Christ after His crucifixion (Acts 20:7). The real question is *why* people gather together on Sunday. Most modern Christians believe that a born-again Christian should go to church on a Sunday to be edified and blessed. This is not strictly true. *First*, a gathering of believers on *any day* of the week is encouraged to build up and edify the Body of Christ and to find peace in your spirit (Hebrews 10:24-25, I Corinthians 14:23,26, Deuteronomy 12:13-14). *Second*, the body of Christ is to gather together to worship and praise God. *Third*, the Saints are to gather together to learn and study the scriptures (Matthew 22:29, Colossians 3:16, Hosea 4:6). The real purpose of gathering together on Sunday or on any other day is to worship God and to praise Him.

The Law continued to dominate the religious and social life of Israel for about another 1,500 years until God sent His only Son Jesus Christ to redeem sinful man and to take away the sins of the world; sins from Adam to the end of time as we know it

Baptism

When Christ began His 3.5-year ministry, the first thing He did in obedience to His father was to be baptized at the Jordan River by John the Baptist. Baptism is the sign of the New Covenant God makes with His Church. Jesus commanded baptism in the Great Commission: *Go therefore and make disciples of all nations, baptizing them*

in the name of the Father and of the Son and of the Holy Spirit (Matthew 28:19). Baptism is the outward sign of an inward change. It represents a new birth into the body of Christ. The Old Covenant had a *physical* means of entrance: one was born to Jewish parents or became a Jew as a *proselyte*. The physical sign that a person or His family was born or assimilated into a true Jewish believer was *circumcision*. However, even the most devoted Jew knew that circumcision of the flesh was not enough. Moses commanded the Israelites to circumcise their *hearts* (Deuteronomy 30:6, 10:16). Jeremiah also preached that every righteous Jew must be circumcised in the heart (Jeremiah 4:4). This circumcision of the heart was to create hope in a long-awaited Messiah who would arise to redeem all of Israel who lived by faith. The act of circumcision in the Old Covenant was replaced by the act of *baptism* in the New Covenant. Note that just like Old Testament circumcision, New Testament baptism never saved anyone. New Testament baptism is a public confirmation of faith. Paul spoke of this mystery in Colossians 2.

[9] *For in him dwelleth all the fulness of the Godhead bodily.*
[10] *And ye are complete in him, which is the head of all principality and power:*
[11] *In whom also ye are circumcised with the circumcision made without hands, in putting off the body of the sins of the flesh by the circumcision of Christ:*
[12] *Buried with him in baptism, wherein also ye are risen with him through the faith of the operation of God, who hath raised him from the dead.*
[13] *And you, being dead in your sins and the uncircumcision of your flesh, hath he quickened together with him, having forgiven you all trespasses.*   Colossians 2:9-13

Many Christians misinterpret the teachings of Christ regarding the concept of being *born again.*

*Jesus answered and said unto him, Verily, verily, I say unto thee, Except a man be **born** again, he cannot see the kingdom of God.*   John 3:3

*Jesus answered, Verily, verily, I say unto thee, Except a man be born of **water** and of the Spirit, he cannot enter into the kingdom of God.*   John 3:5

Putting these two verses together, one can properly interpret John 3:5. The first birth clearly implied on John 3:3 is natural, physical birth, so the second birth implied in John 3:3 must be a birth of another kind. That second birth in John 3:3 is explained in John 3:5 as a spiritual birth. Natural birth is always preceded by a breaking of the woman's water.

The spiritual birth in John 3:5 is what occurs when anyone accepts Jesus Christ as their Lord and Savior. Water baptism is neither the 1ˢᵗ or 2ⁿᵈ birth in John 3:2 and John 3:5.

In John 3, Jesus was talking with Nicodemus, He said; *I tell you the truth, no one can see the kingdom of God unless he is born again.* Nicodemus asked the following question: *How can a man be born when he is old?' Surely he cannot enter a second time into his mother's womb to be born!'* Jesus answered, *I tell you the truth, no one can enter the kingdom of God unless he is born of water and the Spirit. Flesh gives birth to flesh, but the Spirit gives birth to spirit. You should not be surprised at my saying, You must be born again* (John 3:3-7). This should settle the issue.

The Cross

Although once again not specifically called out as a New Covenant *sign*, millions of Christians worldwide and all protestant denominations embrace the *Cross of Calvary* as a sign of Jesus Christ and the work that he accomplished on the cross. It is fitting that the sign of the cross should be an eternal symbol of God's love for us and the sacrificial death of Jesus Christ in obedience to His father in heaven.

The Dispensation of Grace will come to a close when Christ returns at His second advent and fights the battle of Armageddon (Revelation 19). This will be preceded by a great tribulation period in which Satan will make war against Christ, the Jews, and every born-again Christian. Is there a sign that will precede the Tribulation Period? The answer is, *yes*.

War in the Heavenlies

The end of the *Disposition of Grace* will be followed by a 3.5 year worldwide persecution and slaughter of Christians and Jews which has been called the *Great Tribulation*. This 3.5 year period will immediately follow a great war in the heavenlies between Satan and his fallen angels ,and Micheal and his angels. Satan and his angels will be defeated and cast down to earth. This defeat will be immediately followed by the arise of the *Antichrist* and the *False Prophet*: 3.5 years of tribulation will immediately follow. (Phillips, *The Book of Revelation:Mysteries Revealed*) This great hevenly conflict will be seen by everyone on earth and will be a *sign* that the end of the Church Age is near. All prophecy teachers agree that this cosmic conflict will take place 3.5

84

years before the Dispensation of Grace will come to an end. The majority of this 3.5 year period will be the *Seven Trumpet Judgements* which are called the *Wrath of Satan*. The Seven Bowl Judgements are called the *Wrath of God* (Revelation 15:7, 16:1). The Body of Christ has been promised that they will not have to experience the Wrath of God.

He that believeth on the Son hath everlasting life: and he that believeth not the Son shall not see life; but the **wrath** *of God abideth on him*　　　　　　　John 3:36

For the **wrath** *of God is revealed from heaven against all ungodliness and unrighteousness of men, who hold the truth in unrighteousness*　　　Romans 1:18

The same shall drink of the wine of the **wrath** *of God, which is poured out without mixture into the cup of his indignation; and he shall be tormented with fire and brimstone in the presence of the holy angels, and in the presence of the Lamb*
　　　Revelation 14:10

For a complete theological discussion of this battle, see Phillips: The Book of Revelation: *Mysteries Revealed.*

[1] And there appeared a great wonder in heaven; a woman clothed with the sun, and the moon under her feet, and upon her head a crown of twelve stars:
[2] And she being with child cried, travailing in birth, and pained to be delivered.

[3] And there appeared another wonder in heaven; and behold a great red dragon, having seven heads and ten horns, and seven crowns upon his heads.
Revelation 12:1-3
[7] And there was war in heaven: Michael and his angels fought against the dragon; and the dragon fought and his angels,
[8] And prevailed not; neither was their place found any more in heaven.
[9] And the great dragon was cast out, that old serpent, called the Devil, and Satan, which deceivith the whole world: he was cast out into the earth, and his angels were cast out with him.　　　Revelation 12:1-3, 7-9

The Greek word for *wonder* can also be interpreted as a *sign*, and it is interpreted as such in the NIV translation of the Holy Bible. This is the sign that will precede the last 3.5

years of the Age of Grace. This will be a time of great persecution and death whose severity has never been seen before in all of recorded history. All who will not follow after Satan and receive the Mark of the Beast (666) will be martyred. The Rapture of the Church will occur after the seventh trumpet sounds. We will not know the exact time and day of the rapture, but we will know the time and season (Phillips, The Book of Revelation: *Mysteries Revealed*). After the *Wrath of God* (the 7 bowl judgments) falls upon all unbelievers, the great Battle of Armageddon will take place; Satan and his armies will be completely destroyed and the false prophet and the Antichrist will be cast into the *Lake of Fire and Brimstone*. Satan will be cast into the *Bottomless Pit* and the *Great White Throne Judgment* will take place. This will end the Dispensation of Grace.

Peace in the Animal Kingdom

The 1000 year Millennial Dispensation is barely mentioned in the New Testament, and rarely discussed in any Protestant Church congregation. It is a period of time during which the believing Jewish remnant will finally inherit and live on the land promised to Abraham and King David. The Book of Revelation records its beginning and ending, but does not contain any details of the Millennial Kingdom (Revelation 20). However, the Old Testament prophets were given many details of a kingdom on earth in which wonderful things would occur.

Zechariah in Chapters 12 and 13 explain that one-third of all the Jews will survive the Tribulation, finally trust in their Messiah, and enter the Millennium Kingdom. They will repopulate the earth during the Millennium (Matthew 25:31-46; Isaiah 33:24, 35; Psalms 72:16; Micah. 4:7). All those who enter the 1000 year Millennial Kingdom will have accepted Jesus Christ as their savior: , however their offspring will still have a sin nature (Is. 65:20) and have to choose whether to sincerely trust in the Lord. All the Old Testament believers, New Testament church, and Tribulation martyrs will receive their glorified bodies and return with Christ to reign as kings and priests for one thousand years (Exodus 19:6; Daniel 7:13-14; Zechariah 14:5-9; 1 Peter 2:5, 9; Jude 14-15; Revelation 1:6; 5:10; 20:6): *And so **all** Israel shall be saved as it is written* (Romans 11:26). *Sing and rejoice, O daughter of Zion! For behold, I am coming and I will dwell in your midst,' says the LORD. Many nations shall be joined to the LORD in that day, and they shall become My people. And I will dwell in your midst. Then you will know that the LORD of hosts has sent Me to you* (Zechariah. 2:10-11). The Lord Himself will rule and reign from Jerusalem and many nations shall become His people. The animal kingdom will live in peace and harmony throughout the Millennial Kingdom.

*[6] The wolf also shall dwell with the lamb, and the leopard shall lie down with the kid; and the calf and the young **lion** and the fatling together; and a little child shall lead them.*
*[7] And the cow and the bear shall feed; their young ones shall lie down together: and the **lion** shall eat straw like the ox.*   Isaiah 11:6-7

The New Jerusalem

The last age of time will be the Millennial Dispensation. There is no *sign* clearly spoken of in the scriptures, but the 1,000-year millennial kingdom will commence after the Battle of Armageddon. This would be a clear sign to any Jewish believers who are alive and accepted Christ as their long-awaited Messiah. The other sign which will be clearly visible to the nation of Israel who will live in the land promised to Abraham and King David during this 1,000-year period of time will be the *New Jerusalem,* in which all of the raptured saints will inhabit and rule and reign with Christ, Again, this is not a sign which is referred to in the Holy Scriptures, but it should be recognized as a visible fulfillment of the Covenant Promises of God in both the Old and New Testaments. At the end of the Millennial Dispensation, Satan will be loosed for a little while. He will return to the earth and once again gather all unbelievers to him. Stan and his followers will once again march on Jerusalem to wage war. This is the great battle of *Gog and Magog* prophesied in Ezekiel 38-39; but once again Christ will suddenly appear and destroy Satan and all of his followers. The Millennial Dispensation will come to an end by the resurrection of all unbelieving Old Testament Jews and the resurrection of all those who have died during the 1000 year Millennial Dispensation. These two groups will be righteously judged by God at the *Great White Throne Judgment* and condemned to death in the *Lake of Fire*. This is the *Second Death* (Revelation 20:7-15). The last group to be judged will be those who have become believers in the Millennial Kingdom: This is a judgment for rewards and not for salvation (Revelation 20:5).

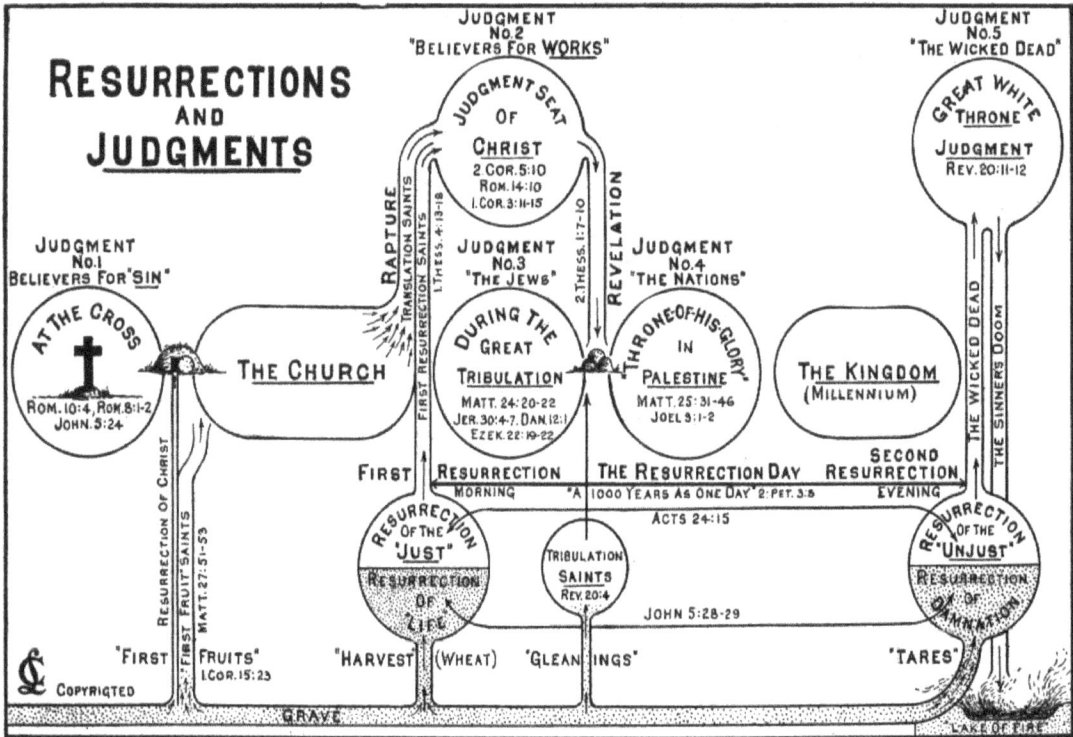

Clarence Larkin (1850-1924)

Part V: The Eternal Plan of Salvation

One of the main reasons for studying the different dispensations and covenant relationships with man across recorded history is to understand the eternal purpose of God in creating man. After God formed the earth (Genesis 1-2), He created the Garden of Eden and populated the earth with animals. Adam was then formed into a *living soul* and placed into the Garden of Eden. Finally, God created Eve as a helpmate for Adam.

[27] *So God created man in his own image, in the image of God created he him; male and female created he them.*
[28] *And God blessed them, and God said unto them, Be fruitful, and multiply, and replenish the earth, and subdue it: and have dominion over the fish of the sea, and over the fowl of the air, and over every living thing that moved upon the earth.*
     Genesis 1: 27-28

This creative act of God set man apart from every other animal, fish, or fowl previously created. Man was placed in the Garden of Eden to live in peace and harmony forever. Their continued existence was made possible by eating of the Tree of Life which grew in the garden. Adam was created in God's own image, and so we are sure that He resembled God in appearance, and his image was the same as man today. The teaching that man and women evolved from apes is a heretic theology and is in direct opposition to the Holy record.

It was God's will that He would commune with man, and this was predicated upon one eternal truth: God can never be in the presence of sin or tolerate sin. Adam and Eve were both sinless and innocent because there was no knowledge of good and evil. As soon as they ate of the tree of the knowledge of good and evil, they knew and experienced sin. Because they had sinned, God expelled them from the Garden of Eden. The entire plan for God's creation then changed. When innocence was lost, Adam and Eve and their subsequent children replenished the earth and lived in what we have called the *Dispensation of Conscience*, since there was no written law. Conscience only comes to man when sin or transgression exists. It is clear that even without any written law, man would inherently know the difference in good and evil. Since there was no written law, there was no transgression of the law, but there was certainly sin and rebellion against God.

Man became so sinful that God could finally stand no more. He spoke to Noah, who was a *righteous man,* and told him to build an *ark* because He was about to destroy the inhabitants of the world by a great flood; and so He did. All perished but a remnant of the animal kingdom and eight people survived the deluge: Noah, his three sons (Shem, Japheth and Ham) and their wives.

God next commanded man to *be fruitful and multiply,* and live in harmony with Him. Man again miserably failed God; and fell into idolatry, sin and idol worship. The apex of man's sinful nature was the construction of the *Tower of Babel* in the Land of Shinar, led by a man named *Nimrod.* The purpose of this structure was to elevate the people above the earth so they could be *like God.* In righteous indignation, God destroyed the Tower of Babel, scattered the people about the earth and *confused* their languages. In spite of being scattered across the earth and experiencing God's wrath, man once again followed after their own desires and failed God. But God is *longsuffering* and He still had a desire to commune and interact with mankind; so He once again intervened.

God called *Abram* out of Ur of the Chaldee to begin a new nation of people called *Israel.* Israel was to be God's chosen people. He would bless them, protect them and promised them an inheritance of land. However, in spite of all their blessings they eventually would lose faith and move to Egypt where they became slaves to the Egyptian Pharaoh. The Children of Israel spent a total of 215 years in Egypt after spending 215 years in the Land of Canaan. Exactly 430 years after God had called Abram out of the Ur of Chaldee, He heard their cries and raised up His servant Moses to lead them out of bondage. At Mt. Sinai, exactly 50 days after Moses had led the Exodus from Egypt, God gave His people a set of 10 commandments and 613 laws governing their religious, social and dietary behavior. This began of the *Dispensation the Law* which lasted over 1,500 years until Christ initiated the *Dispensation of Grace.*

In the fullness of time God sent His only Son to redeem mankind, and he would be called Jesus. In Jesus all of the promises given to Adam, Noah, Abraham, and Moses would reside in Christ the Messiah. Since the beginning of time, God had preordained his only Son to take away the sins of the world. Christ began His earthly ministry of 3.5 years in the Hebrew month of Tishri (September/October) in 30 AD. It was likely on or very near the Feast of Tabernacles when John the Baptizer looked down a long dusty road at the River Jordan where he was preaching repentance and baptizing the people.

...John saw Jesus coming unto him, and said, Behold the Lamb of God, which taketh away the sin of the world.   John 1:29

To the casual western-world reader, this may seem to be only poetic, descriptive language; but to the Jews of that time it would have been a prophetic and astounding statement by John the Baptist.

The average Christian has not bothered to closely study the Old Testament and see how everything which took place in the Old Testament scriptures was in some way linked to Jesus Christ, the Son of God. There is much confusion and lack of knowledge in the Body of Christ concerning how people were saved in the Old Testament. The key issue is sin. God is holy and perfect, and He cannot coexist with any man or woman that is stained with sin. It is this very fact that the innocence and sinless nature of Adam and Eve allowed God to walk with them in the *cool of the evening.* When Adam and Eve ate of the fruit of the Tree of Knowledge between good and evil they sinned against God who commanded them not to do so. Because of this sin, Adam and Eve were cast from the Garden of Eden. This act of disobedience by both Adam and Eve not only changed their existence in the Garden of Eden, but also changed their fundamental relationship with God and the state of man from that point on. Since Adam was corrupted by sin, every man, woman and child which would ever exist was also corrupted. This is because all of mankind sprang from the loins and seed of Adam. There is a very important concept which has being given to us from creation: Some have called this the *Law of Genesis. Everything will reproduce after its own kind.* In other words, a cat doesn't come from a dog. A watermelon doesn't come from an orange. Everything that God created comes from and reproduces after its own kind. Because Adam possessed the *sin nature* when he violated God's commandment, that sin nature would be passed on to all who would follow him. The sin nature is that principle in man that makes him rebellious against God. When we speak of the sin nature, we refer to the fact that we have a natural inclination to sin. We have been created by God to obey His commandments, but God has given us the *free will* to choose sin or righteousness. Given the choice to do God's will or follow after our own desires, mankind will naturally choose to do his own thing. The Bible speaks of *sinful flesh* in Romans 8:3, and it is our *own desire* to follow earthly pleasures that produces the list of sins in Colossians 3:5. Paul in Romans 6:6 speaks of *the body ruled by sin.* The flesh-and-blood existence we lead on this earth is shaped by our sinful, corrupt nature inherited from Adam.

Sin is a part of the very fiber of our being, it is what separates us from God and His blessings. However, we must be very clear that it can never separate us from the love of God. Ultimately, God so loved the world that He sent His only begotten son to take away the sins of the world on the Cross of Calvary. It is not commonly well-understood that the last words which Christ spoke from the cross were, *It is finished*. These words were profound and deep. When Christ died on the cross, He finished His work and did three things that only the Son of God could accomplish:

(1) Christ Abolished the Curse of the Law

The Old Testament Laws were given to Moses and the Children of Israel to both separate themselves from the other people in the world and to protect them spiritually, physically and nutritionally. The Apostle Paul made it quite clear in the Book of Romans that the law was never meant to save mankind, but to serve as a taskmaster which clearly pointed out the inability of man to follow the will of God.

*Therefore by the deeds of the **law** there shall no flesh be justified in his sight: for by the **law** is the knowledge of sin.*   Romans 3:20

*Because the **law** worketh wrath: for where no **law** is, there is no transgression.*
Romans 4:15

*Knowing that a man is not justified by the works of the **law**, but by the faith of Jesus Christ, even we have believed in Jesus Christ, that we might be justified by the faith of Christ, and not by the works of the **law**: for by the works of the **law** shall no flesh be justified.*   Galatians 2:16

*For whosoever shall keep the whole law, and yet offend in one point, he is guilty of **all**.*
James 2:10

Without permanent forgiveness of sin, the law condemned and killed. This is why the Law, which was written on tablets of stone, needed to be replaced by laws that were written on the heart. However, it must be clearly understood that the Laws of Moses given to the people at Mt. Sinai are *still in effect*. The Laws that Moses received at Mt. Sinai were given by God and they are still holy and good. The law condemned because breaking the law was a sin, but when Christ came, the sin of violating the law would be forgiven by the sacrificial death of Jesus Christ. The laws which were written on *stone* would now be written on the *heart*. Of course, this does not mean that in the *Dispensation of Grace* any born-again Christian could purposely violate any Old Testament law; Paul addressed this issue in his epistles.

*Is the law then against the promises of **God**? **God** forbid: for if there had been a law given which could have given life, verily righteousness should have been by the law.*
    Galatians 3:21

*Do we then make void the law through faith? **God** forbid: yea, we establish the law.*
    Romans 3:21

*What then? shall we sin, because we are not under the law, but under grace? **God** forbid.*
    Romans 6:15

(2) Jesus Christ Settled the Sin Issue on the Cross of Calvary

The sin issue was settled on the Cross of Calvary as a barrier which prevented man from entering into the Kingdom of Heaven and God's Holy presence.

It should now be clear that the issue of sin, specifically the forgiveness of sin, had to be settled to reconcile man to God. The eternal plan of God is now completely understood. When Adam and Eve sinned, they were physically and spiritually separated from God, and there was no way to forgive their sin because Jesus Christ had not yet appeared. When any person in the *Dispensation of Conscience* or the *Noahidic Dispensation* died, they died in sin, both because of the inherited sin nature from Adam and by their own, willful transgressions against the natural laws of God. When Cain slew his brother Abel, did he break one of God's Laws? No, there was no written law. Did he sin? Yes, and God passed judgment on him personally and drove him into the wilderness. Did Abraham sin at any time? Yes, *For all have sinned and fallen short of the Glory of God.* Did Moses the faithful servant of God sin? Yes, and God also passed judgment upon him: he was not allowed to enter into the promised land. So Cain, Abraham and Moses were all doomed to physical and spiritual death because of sin. But God has always had an eternal plan to redeem sinful man.

After the law was given at Mt. Sinai, every Jew from then until now broke the law, and Paul said that if *one breaks only one part of the law, he has broken the whole law*! But was it not true that under the Law of Moses, a Levitical sacrificial system was ordained and put in place by God to provide for the forgiveness of sin? NO. The Levitical sacrificial system was only a shadow and type of the accomplished work of Jesus Christ. The sacrifice of bulls and goats, and the ritual of sprinkling blood upon the horns of the Altar of Sacrifice were only an *atonement* for sin.

For it is not possible that the blood of bulls and of goats should take away sins.
Hebrews 10:4

The word *atonement* in the Old Testament never conveyed the concept of permanent forgiveness of sin(s). Atonement, in the Hebrew, means a *covering*. The Levitical sacrificial system was never meant to permanently forgive sins, but to only temporarily allow the transgressor to continue in a relationship with God.

It then follows that if man was to be reconciled to God and receive the award of eternal life, the sins of man would need to be forever forgiven and forgotten. No mortal man could ever accomplish that, only God himself could. He did so by sending His only Son down from heaven to be the perfect sacrificial lamb. The Law was a taskmaster which was intended to show man that it was impossible to live a sinless life under the law, and that if man was a hopeless sinner lost in transgressions there would need to be a deliverer which would arise who could permanently forgive sins. Since man could never accomplish such a thing, a redeemer would need to be sent who would come directly from God. In order to abolish the curse of the law, but not to take away its intent, Christ left His seat in the heavenlies next to God the Father and came to earth as God in the flesh. Christ was all man and all God sent from the Father. Christ was the only person who ever walked the face of the earth that lived a sinless life under all of the law. He was born a Jew, lived a Jew, and died a Jew. Jesus repeatedly proclaimed that He walked as the *Son of Man*, and affirmed that He was sent to satisfy every commandment of the law.

[17] *Think not that I am come to destroy the law, or the prophets: I am not come to destroy, but to fulfil.*
[18] *For verily I say unto you, Till heaven and earth pass, one jot or one tittle shall in no wise pass from the law, till all be fulfilled.*   Matthew 5:17-18

(3) Christ established a New Covenant by Which All People Would be Saved By Faith and not Works.

Jesus Christ further confirmed that the spirit and intent of the law would never pass away until all that was prophesied in the scriptures would come to pass. Christ made it clear that He was not sent to destroy the Law, but to fulfill the Law. *Why?* Because Christ had to be perfect in every way and sinless. Only a sinless redeemer could offer Himself up as the perfect and final sacrificial lamb. John the Baptist prophesied of that finished work on the Cross of Calvary when he said, *Behold the Lamb of God who taketh away the sins of the world.* Our Lord Jesus Christ satisfied every aspect of the Law, because He had to be accepted by the Father as sinless. He was freed from the curse of Adam by being born into this world through the pure and sinless seed of God the Father, and He subjected

Himself to all of the sorrows and temptations of man by being born in the flesh. Because He was blameless and without sin, He was the perfect sacrifice for sin. But, Christ did not die on the cross as the sinless *Lamb of God* for Himself. He died for the sins of the entire world: past, present and future. Because of His personal and obedient sacrificial death on the cross of Calvary, the entire playing field of man in sin was abolished. Salvation would be freely offered to both Jews and Gentiles alike after Christ died on the cross. If sin was permanently forgiven at the cross, then there was and is only one barrier left to attain eternal life: Salvation is now based upon only one thing, *FAITH*. Faith that Jesus Christ was the Son of God who came, lived and died for each individual who had ever lived and will ever live. His precious blood that was shed covered every sin. The great theme of the New Covenant is that salvation is now freely offered to all by grace and not by works, *lest any man should boast*. Salvation is imputed by *faith*, and by faith alone. The eternal plan of God should now be clear. Every man or woman that ever lived or will ever live from Adam and Eve until the end of time will be saved in exactly the same way, by faith. Both before and after our Lord Jesus Christ died on the cross of Calvary salvation is freely offered to all who will believe upon His name. No one deserves to be saved and spend eternity in the presence of God; our salvation is by grace and faith. A common misconception about salvation in the Old Testament is that Jews were saved by keeping the Law: This could never have been possible.

[6] Even as Abraham believed God, and it was accounted to him for righteousness.
[7] Know ye therefore that they which are of faith, the same are the children of Abraham.
[8] And the scripture, foreseeing that God would justify the heathen through faith, preached before the gospel unto Abraham, saying, In thee shall all nations be blessed.
[9] So then they which be of faith are blessed with faithful Abraham.
[10] For as many as are of the works of the law are under the curse: for it is written, Cursed is every one that continueth not in all things which are written in the book of the law to do them.
[11] But that no man is justified by the law in the sight of God, it is evident: for, The just shall live by faith.
[12] And the law is not of faith: but, The man that doeth them shall live in them.
[13] Christ hath redeemed us from the curse of the law, being made a curse for us
            Galatians 3:6-13

Some might want to dismiss this passage as applying only to the New Testament, but Paul is quoting Habakkuk 2:4. Salvation by faith was an *Old Testament* principle. The remaining problem which must be resolved is that in Old Testament times no one knew Jesus Christ by name and no one knew that He would be the long-awaited Jewish Messiah who would take away their sins. The resolution of this problem can only be found by carefully studying the Old Testament and rightly dividing the Word of God. When Adam and Eve fell from a sinless existence in the Garden of Eden, God immediately gave the first prophecy recorded in the holy scriptures.

And I will put enmity between thee and the woman, and between thy seed and her seed; it shall bruise thy head, and thou shalt bruise his heel.   Genesis 3:15

This prophecy to Adam and Eve has been debated and interpreted by many biblical scholars, and we will not attempt to provide a complete interpretation. However, even a casual reading of this passage will reveal the basic intent. The phrase, *her seed*, is referring to offspring from Eve. As women do not have the male seed, Genesis 3:15 gives us a hint of the special and unique birth of the coming one that would *bruise the head* of Satan, defeating sin and death and providing a way of atonement for all that accept His coming (past and future) by faith. The passage is addressed to *Satan* in the form of a serpent, and from this point on there would be enmity (spiritual war) between mankind and Satan. The *seed* of Satan is not a natural offspring, but those fallen angels who are called *sons of Satan*; her seed referred to Jesus Christ who was born of the woman, Mary. Jesus Christ (it) would come and bruise *thy head* (Satan) but *thou* (Satan) would bruise *His* (Jesus Christ) hccl on the Cross of Calvary. It is almost certain that when God spoke this to Adam and Eve, they asked for an explanation. Even today after almost 6,000 years, theologians still debate this passage. It is consistent with God's eternal plan to have His Son redeem mankind by faith. Adam and Eve probably had a vague idea of how they were to be redeemed, but just like all Old Testament believers they only had a partial picture of the future. It was not recorded in the book of Genesis, but it is certain that they were told to have faith in a future redeemer if their sins were to be forgiven; it would be faith in a messiah who would arise thousands of years later that would forgive their sins. They certainly understood that this redeemer would arise from one of their descendants.

God would not further reveal His redemptive plan for mankind until almost 2,000 years later when He made a covenant relationship with Abram and changed his name to Abraham. Just like Adam and Eve, Abraham knew that he had sinned and needed a redeemer who would be sent by God and forgive his sins. And he (Abraham) ***believed in the LORD***; and he counted it to him for **righteousness** (Genesis 15:6).

God expanded upon His prophecy which was given to Adam and Eve, and gave Abraham more details about the promised Messiah.

And I will bless them that bless thee, and curse him that curseth thee: and in thee shall all families of the earth be blessed.   Genesis 12:3

*And, behold, I establish my covenant with you, and with your **seed** after you;*   Genesis 12:9

Paul in Galatians revealed that Abraham was told that his seed would produce the promised Messiah who would take away the sins of the world.

Now to Abraham and his seed were the promises made. He saith not, And to seeds, as of many; but as of one, And to thy seed, which is Christ.   Galatians 3:16

Adam and Eve only knew that the promised Messiah who would *bruise the head of Satan* would be from his progeny. Abraham was told that from all of the people and nations that had sprung from Adam, the promised Messiah would come from his family line and one of the 12 tribes of Israel. Just like Adam, Abraham would never see Christ but by faith he believed that He would someday arise. *And he believed in the Lord, and he counted it to him for righteousness* (Genesis 15:6). Many years later, God visited King David and revealed to him that the long-awaited Messiah would someday arise from his line, the throne of David would be established forever, and the long-awaited Messiah would come from the tribe of Judah. In another remarkable prophecy given to the prophet Micah, it was revealed that He would be born in the city of Bethlehem.

But you, Bethlehem Ephrathah, though you are little among the thousands of Judah, yet out of you shall come forth to Me the One to be Ruler in Israel, Whose goings forth are from of old, from everlasting.   Micah 5:2

Christ Fulfilled All Old Testament Prophecies Concerning Him
There are many passages where the Old Testament clearly speaks about the Messiah who would one day come to the world. These passages are so clear, that Jews and Christians are in agreement that they describe the Messiah. In the Old Testament, the only thing that was hidden from the Jewish people was the name *Jesus* of the Messiah that would someday arise to not only forgive all of their sins, but the sins of the whole world….Jews and Gentiles alike. Although the prophesied Jewish Messiah was never called Jesus in the Old Testament, the Nation of Israel and the Jewish believers had no excuse whatsoever of not believing that when Jesus Christ appeared in 26 AD that He had to be their long awaited redeemer and messiah. Throughout the Old Testament, the identity and characteristics of Jesus Christ were *progressively revealed*. Some biblical scholars identify over 100 direct or indirect prophesies recorded in the scriptures that could only

describe Jesus Christ of Nazareth. We will list only 44 Messianic prophecies which were fulfilled by the coming of Christ.

	44 Prophecies Jesus Christ Fulfilled		
	Prophecies About Jesus	**Old Testament Scripture**	**New Testament Fulfillment**
1	Messiah would be born of a woman.	Genesis 3:15	Matthew 1:20 Galatians 4:4
2	Messiah would be born in Bethlehem.	Micah 5:2	Matthew 2:1 Luke 2:4-6
3	Messiah would be born of a virgin.	Isaiah 7:14	Matthew 1:22-23 Luke 1:26-31
4	Messiah would come from the line of Abraham.	Genesis 12:3 Genesis 22:18	Matthew 1:1 Romans 9:5
5	Messiah would be a descendant of Isaac.	Genesis 17:19 Genesis 21:12	Luke 3:34
6	Messiah would be a descendant of Jacob.	Numbers 24:17	Matthew 1:2
7	Messiah would come from the tribe of Judah.	Genesis 49:10	Luke 3:33 Hebrews 7:14
8	Messiah would be heir to King David's throne.	2 Samuel 7:12-13 Isaiah 9:7	Luke 1:32-33 Romans 1:3
9	Messiah's throne will be anointed and eternal.	Psalm 45:6-7 Daniel 2:44	Luke 1:33 Hebrews 1:8-12
10	Messiah would be called Immanuel.	Isaiah 7:14	Matthew 1:23
11	Messiah would spend a season in Egypt.	Hosea 11:1	Matthew 2:14-15
12	A massacre of children at Messiah's birthplace.	Jeremiah 31:15	Matthew 2:16-18

13	A messenger would prepare the way for Messiah	Isaiah 40:3-5	Luke 3:3-6
14	Messiah would be rejected by his own people.	Psalm 69:8 Isaiah 53:3	John 1:11 John 7:5
15	Messiah would be a prophet.	Deuteronomy 18:15	Acts 3:20-22
16	Messiah would be preceded by Elijah.	Malachi 4:5-6	Matthew 11:13-14
17	Messiah would be declared the Son of God.	Psalm 2:7	Matthew 3:16-17
18	Messiah would be called a Nazarene.	Isaiah 11:1	Matthew 2:23
19	Messiah would bring light to Galilee.	Isaiah 9:1-2	Matthew 4:13-16
20	Messiah would speak in parables.	Psalm 78:2-4 Isaiah 6:9-10	Matthew 13:10-15, 34-35
21	Messiah would be sent to heal the brokenhearted.	Isaiah 61:1-2	Luke 4:18-19
22	Messiah would be a priest after the order of Melchizedek.	Psalm 110:4	Hebrews 5:5-6
23	Messiah would be called King.	Psalm 2:6 Zechariah 9:9	Matthew 27:37 Mark 11:7-11
24	Messiah would be praised by little children.	Psalm 8:2	Matthew 21:16
25	Messiah would be betrayed.	Psalm 41:9 Zechariah 11:12-13	Luke 22:47-48 Matthew 26:14-16
26	Messiah's price money would be used to buy a potter's field.	Zechariah 11:12-13	Matthew 27:9-10
27	Messiah would be falsely accused.	Psalm 35:11	Mark 14:57-58

28	Messiah would be silent before his accusers.	Isaiah 53:7	Mark 15:4-5
29	Messiah would be spat upon and struck.	Isaiah 50:6	Matthew 26:67
30	Messiah would be hated without cause.	Psalm 35:19 Psalm 69:4	John 15:24-25
31	Messiah would be crucified with criminals.	Isaiah 53:12	Matthew 27:38 Mark 15:27-28
32	Messiah would be given vinegar to drink.	Psalm 69:21	Matthew 27:34 John 19:28-30
33	Messiah's hands and feet would be pierced.	Psalm 22:16 Zechariah 12:10	John 20:25-27
34	Messiah would be mocked and ridiculed.	Psalm 22:7-8	Luke 23:35
37	Messiah would be forsaken by God.	Psalm 22:1	Matthew 27:46
38	Messiah would pray for his enemies.	Psalm 109:4	Luke 23:34
39	Soldiers would pierce Messiah's side.	Zechariah 12:10	John 19:34
40	Messiah would be buried with the rich.	Isaiah 53:9	Matthew 27:57-60
41	Messiah would resurrect from the dead.	Psalm 16:10 Psalm 49:15	Matthew 28:2-7 Acts 2:22-32
42	Messiah would ascend to heaven.	Psalm 24:7-10	Mark 16:19
43	Messiah would be seated at God's right hand.	Psalm 68:18 Psalm 110:1	Mark 16:19 Matthew 22:44
44	Messiah would be a sacrifice for sin.	Isaiah 53:5-12	Romans 5:6-8

(Source: 100 Prophecies Fulfilled by Jesus: Messianic Prophecies Made Before the Birth of Christ by Rose Publishing; **Book of Bible Lists** by H.L. Wilmington; NKJV Study Bible; Life Application Study Bible.)

We now arrive at the answer to perhaps the most-important question that can ever be asked concerning the millions of people who lived and died before Christ arrived as the promised Messiah. *How did the **Old Testament men and women**, including the Jews, obtain salvation and eternal life if they all died in sin*? The other question to be asked is: *How do **New Covenant** men and women, including Jews, obtain salvation and eternal life?* The answer to both questions should now be understood to be *exactly* the same. Both groups of people are saved in the same way, *by faith*. The scriptures are quite clear that both groups of people only obtain salvation by believing in faith that a redeemer would arise that would take away the sins of the entire world.

All the Old Testament saints died in sin, but by faith they believed that someday God would send a redeemer who would take away their sins, never to be remembered; and that by faith alone reward their faith with eternal life. Salvation has always been offered by grace and not by works. Every New Testament saint is saved by believing that in 30 AD Jesus Christ, the Son of God, was crucified on the cross of Calvary and took away the sins of each individual who would believe upon Him by faith. Every Old Testament Jew was saved by faith and grace, just as every New Testament believer is saved by grace and faith. The difference is that every Old Testament believer looked *forward* through time to the cross and every New Testament believer looks *backward* to the cross.

Another key difference is that the redeemer promised to Old Testament saints was predicted and prophesied without knowing His name, but the person of Christ and His appearance was well-known and understood. New Testament Saints have the work and appearance of Christ recorded in the four gospels and the epistles of the apostles. However, the actual personage of Jesus Christ was only seen in person over a short time. He died at 33.5 years of age after a 3.5-year ministry. However, even during that time period, Jews and Gentiles that walked the earth with Christ were also saved by faith. Christ spent His entire earthly ministry proclaiming with signs and miracles that He was the Son of God sent to take away the sins of the world and offer salvation by faith and grace. The Pharisees, Sadducees and the Jewish Priesthood all rejected His claims and failed to accept Him as teir long-awaited and promised Messiah.. It was this same lack of faith and discernment that finally led them to crucify Him at Calvary. Jesus Christ the Son of God said:

*Jesus saith unto him, I am the **way**, the truth, and the life: no man cometh unto the Father, but by me.*   John 14:6

*I am the **door**: by me if any man enter in, he shall be saved, and shall go in and out, and find pasture.*   John 10:9

*He that believeth on me, as the scripture hath said, out of his belly shall flow rivers of **living** water.*   John 7:38

*And whosoever liveth and believeth in me shall **never** die. Believest thou this?*   John 11:26

*For therein is the righteousness of God revealed from **faith** to **faith**: as it is written, The just shall live by **faith**.*   Romans 1:17

*[27] Where is boasting then? It is excluded. By what law? of works? Nay: but by the law of **faith**.*
*[28] Therefore we conclude that a man is justified by **faith** without the deeds of the law.*
[30] Seeing it is one God, which shall justify the circumcision by faith, and uncircumcision through faith   Romans 3:27-30

Every person that ever lived before and after Jesus Christ died on the Cross of Calvary committed sin: *For all have sinned, and come **short** of the glory of God* (Romans 3:23). Old Testament men and women died in sin, because their long-awaited Messiah who would take away and forgive their sins had not yet appeared. So what happened to these people at death? In the Hebrew Scriptures, the word used to describe the realm of the dead is called *Sheol*. It means the *place of the dead* or the *place of departed souls*. The Greek New Testament equivalent to Sheol is *hades*. Sheol is often translated *Hell*, and hell is usually associated with a place of torments. This is unfortunate, because when Sheol is interpreted as hell it fails to identify the place where one's soul dwelled after death. Sheol is divided into two compartments: a place called *paradise,* and a place called *torments*. When an Old Testament person died, their soul was immediately taken to paradise if they died in faith like Abraham, and the soul of an unbeliever was taken to a place called torments. The souls residing in paradise were there by faith in the coming, promised Messiah who would take away their sins. The souls residing in the place of torments had died as unbelievers and await their final judgment and sentencing at the Great White Throne Judgment following the 1,000-year millennial kingdom.

Jacob said:

For I will go down into the grave (Sheol) unto my son mourning.   Genesis 37:35

The Apostle Paul said: *The rich man also died, and was buried, and in hell (Hades) he lift up his eyes, being in torments.*   Luke 16:22-23

King David said: *For thou wilt not leave my soul in hell (Sheol); neither wilt thou suffer thine Holy One to see corruption.*   Psalm 16:10

Further proof of this is seen when we realize what Jesus Christ did after He breathed His last breath on the Cross of Calvary.

[9] *(Now that he ascended, what is it but that he also **descended** first into the lower parts of the earth?*
[10] *He that **descended** is the same also that ascended up far above all heavens, that he might fill all things.)*   Ephesians 4:9-10

We confirm that Christ descended into hell (*Sheol*) upon His death for three days and three nights following His sacrificial death every time we recite the Apostles Creed.

> *I believe in God, the Father Almighty, Creator of Heaven and earth;*
> *and in Jesus Christ, His only Son Our Lord, Who was conceived by the Holy Spirit,*
> *born of the Virgin Mary, suffered under Pontius Pilate, was crucified, died, and was*
> *buried. **He descended into Hell**; the third day He rose again from the dead;*
> *He ascended into Heaven, and sitteth at the right hand of God, the Father almighty;*
> *from thence He shall come to judge the living and the dead.*

If most Christians associate *hell* with a single place of torments, why did Christ descend into its depths? Christ immediately descended into the *compartment* of Hell called *paradise* to tell the Old Testament saints who had died in faith that He was their long-awaited Messiah. The Lord's body was placed into the tomb of Joseph (Matthew 27:59-60), but His soul went to Sheol/Hades:

.... thou wilt not leave my soul in hell (Hades), neither wilt thou suffer thine Holy One to see corruption.   Acts 2:27

This is strong confirmation that King David, by divine revelation, understood that he would go to a place called Hades at death and remain there until Christ came. The soul of Christ went to Hades but He was there for only three days and three nights. Peter gives further explanation:

He (David) seeing this before, spake of the resurrection of Christ, that His soul was not left in hell (Hades), neither his flesh did see corruption.   Acts 2:31

Christ's soul was in Sheol/Hades between His death and resurrection. The place where Christ's soul went between His death and resurrection was *paradise* (Luke 23:43). Christ promised the thief on the cross that on that very day he would be with Him in paradise. After Christ preached the gospel message and good news for three days and three nights, He ascended to the Father. The narrative in Luke 16:19–31 proves that prior to Christ's resurrection Hades was divided into two realms: a place of comfort where Lazarus was being held (Paradise or Abraham's bosom), and a place of torment where the rich man was being held.

[20] *And there was a certain beggar named Lazarus, which was laid at his gate, full of sores,*
[21] *And desiring to be fed with the crumbs which fell from the rich man's table: moreover the dogs came and licked his sores.*
[22] *And it came to pass, that the beggar died, and was carried by the angels into Abraham's bosom: the rich man also died, and was buried;*
[23] *And in hell he lift up his eyes, being in torments, and seeth Abraham afar off, and Lazarus in his bosom.*
[24] *And he cried and said, Father Abraham, have mercy on me, and send Lazarus, that he may dip the tip of his finger in water, and cool my tongue; for I am tormented in this flame.*
[25] *But Abraham said, Son, remember that thou in thy lifetime receivedst thy good things, and likewise Lazarus evil things: but now he is comforted, and thou art tormented.*
[26] *And beside all this, between us and you there is a great gulf fixed: so that they which would pass from hence to you cannot; neither can they pass to us, that would come from thence*   Luke 16:20-26

 Lazarus's place of comfort is identical to *paradise* (Luke 23:43). Between the two abodes of the dead there was *a great chasm* (Luke 16:26). The fact that no one could cross this chasm indicates that after death one's fate is sealed. Note that three days after Jesus told the thief that he would be in Paradise with Him, He told Mary Magdalene, who first saw Him in resurrected form; *Do not cling to me, for I have not yet ascended to the My Father* (John 20:17). If He had not yet ascended to His Father, then *Paradise was not located in heaven.* In fact, Ephesians 4:10 states that Christ *descended* into hell.

[8] *Wherefore he saith, When he **ascended** up on high, he led captivity captive, and gave gifts unto men.*
[9] *(Now that he ascended, what is it but that he also **descended first** into the lower parts*

of the earth?

[10] He that descended is the same also that ascended up far above all heavens, that he might fill all things.)   Ephesians 4:8-10

It appears that Christ moved Paradise from the depths of the earth (down) into the presence of God (up). He evidently also moved *captives* who had been residing in Paradise into the very presence of God.

The Apostle Paul was allowed to visit and see paradise while He was alive. He referred to himself as simply *a man.*

I know a man in Christ who fourteen years ago—whether in the body I do not know, or out of the body I do not know, God knows—such a man was caught up to the third heaven. And I know how such a man—whether in the body or apart from the body I do not know, God knows—was caught up into Paradise and heard inexpressible words, which a man is not permitted to speak.   Corinthians 12:2–4

It is certainly inferred from Ephesians 4:8-10 and II Corinthians 12:2-4 that paradise was *moved* from the depths of the earth to the presence of God. This is thought to be true since Paul recorded that he had *ascended* into the third heaven and saw paradise there.

Today, when an *unbeliever* dies, he or she joins the Old Testament unbelievers in the *torments* side of Sheol. At the final judgment, all souls residing there will be taken to the *Great White Throne Judgment*, where its occupants will be judged prior to being cast into the lake of fire (Revelation 20:13–15). All *believers* will also be judged, but not for punishment, for rewards. This will take place at the *Bema Seat Judgment* immediately following the *resurrection* of all dead saints and the *rapture* of all those who remain alive. I believe that when anyone who is a part of the *ekklesia* and has died since the cross enters into this special place still called paradise in the *presence of the Lord.* There is one strong and compelling reason for believing that this must be true. Anyone who has accepted Jesus Christ as their personal Savior will be *rewarded* at the Bema Seat Judgment, and this will not take place until the Age of Grace has come to an end and the Rapture occurs. It does not make sense to me that anyone would be roaming around heaven and serving the Lord *before* he/she is rewarded at the Bema Seat with eternal tasks to execute with our Lord Jesus Christ. I therefore conclude that when a true believer whose sins are already forgiven by the work of Christ at Calvary, and has been born again by Faith in Jesus Christ, will wait in a wonderful, peaceful place which Paul saw and called *Paradise,* where each resident will peacefully await his/her eternal rewards. This is still a *mystery*, since Paul was not allowed to reveal what he had seen.

It is almost universally taught that when a true believer dies, the soul of the departed is immediately taken into the third heaven (an exception is the belief that an intermediate place called *purgatory* exists, which has no scriptural basis whatsoever). The belief that when a true believer dies they go directly to heaven has no *solid* scriptural basis except in something that Paul wrote in II Corinthians.

[6] *…we are always confident, knowing that, whilst we are at home in the body, we are absent from the Lord:*
[7] *(For we walk by faith, not by sight:)*
[8] *We are confident, I say, and willing rather to be absent from the body, and to be present with the Lord.*   II Corinthians 5:6–8

Note carefully that there is no *immediacy* in Paul's statement. He is simply saying that he would rather be present with the Lord than to be in this earthly tabernacle. It is much like someone saying; *I would rather be fishing than to be at work today.* In this place called Paradise which now exists in the third heaven, all New Covenant believers join all of the Old Testament saints who were saved by **faith** and await the second advent of Jesus Christ.

*And will be a Father unto you, and ye shall be **my** sons and daughters, saith the Lord Almighty.*   II Corinthians 6:18

106

Summary and Conclusions

The questions of how all Old Testament believers were saved and what happened to them when they died have been answered with some degree of confidence. The Old Testament believers were all saved by *faith* just as all Christians are saved today. It is certain that born again Christians today have never seen Jesus Christ and never talked with Him personally. Salvation is and has always been by *faith*.

*To open their eyes, and to turn them from darkness to light, and from the power of Satan unto God, that they may receive forgiveness of sins, and inheritance among them which are sanctified by **faith** that is in me.*   Acts 26:18

*Therefore we conclude that a man is justified by **faith** without the deeds of the* law.
                              Romans 3:28

*Therefore we conclude that a man is justified by **faith** without the deeds of the law.*
                              Romans 4:5

[1]   *Therefore being justified by **faith**, we have peace with God through our Lord Jesus Christ:*
[2]   *By whom also we have access by **faith** into this grace wherein we stand, and rejoice in hope of the glory of God.*   Romans 5:1-2

*[26] But now is made manifest, and by the scriptures of the prophets, according to the commandment of the everlasting God, made known to all nations for the obedience of **faith**:*   Romans 16:26

*Knowing that a man is not justified by the works of the law, but by the **faith** of Jesus Christ, even we have believed in Jesus Christ, that we might be justified by the **faith** of Christ, and not by the works of the law: for by the works of the law shall no flesh be justified.*   Galatians 2:16

*Know ye therefore that they which are of **faith**, the same are the children of Abraham.*
                              Galatians 3:7

*[23] But before **faith** came, we were kept under the law, shut up unto the **faith** which should afterwards be revealed.*
*[24] Wherefore the law was our schoolmaster to bring us unto Christ, that we might be justified by **faith**.*
*[25] But after that **faith** is come, we are no longer under a schoolmaster.*

*[26] For ye are all the children of God by **faith** in Christ Jesus.*   Galatians 3:23-26

It has been shown with some confidence that all Old Testament saints who died believing in faith that a Messiah would someday arise and redeem them from sin went to a compartment of Sheol called *paradise.* All Old Testament unbelievers went to a compartment of Sheol called the *place of torments.* There they await their final judgment at the *Great White Throne* which will immediately follow the 1,000-year *Millennial Dispensation.*

It is clear that all Old Testament saints who lived and died by faith looking for the appearance of a future Messiah were all saved in exactly the same way that all true believers of faith in the *Dispensation of Grace* are saved today. Although both groups lived under a different dispensation, the eternal plan of God for mankind has never changed. *Christ was slain from the foundation of the world* (Ephesians 1:4).

It is my belief that the *ekklesia* (which means the *chosen ones*) is composed of believers from Adam to the Rapture. They were not *pre-chosen* at birth but were all saved by **faith.** We should try to clarify what is meant by the following verse.

*If ye were of the world, the world would love his own: but because ye are not of the world, but I have **chosen** you out of the world, therefore the world hateth you.*
John 15:19

In the Book of Revelation, the Apostle John observed a conflict between the *beast* (Antichrist) and an earthly 10 nation confederacy who will fight against the lamb (Christ) during the last 3.5 years of the Great Tribulation period.

*These (10 nations) shall make war with the Lamb (Jesus Christ), and the Lamb shall overcome them: for he is Lord of lords, and King of kings: and they that are with him are **called**, and **chosen**, and **faithful.*** Revelation 17:14

What did Christ mean when He called those that were with Him called, chosen and faithful?
> ***Called***…. The Greek word for *called* is ***kletos***, which means "a calling of Man to accept Jesus Christ as their personal Savior" (Vines Bible Dictionary)
> ***Chosen***… The Greek word for *chosen* is ***eklektos***, which means "chosen out or selected" (Vines Bible Dictionary)
> ***Faithful***…. The Greek word for faithful is ***pistos***, which means " trusted, active, reliable" (Vines Bible Dictionary)

God allows human beings to make their own decisions regarding Him and what He has done for us. And what He has done is to die for the sins of *everyone*. He *chose* to do so and it pleased Him to do so in spite of the suffering that He endured. The Holy Spirit and Christ calls all to salvation. Every person that is alive now on this earth on has been *called* to have salvation. It is written that *many are called but few are chosen* (Matthew 22:14. We could theologically debate this statement for many pages, but note that the mere fact that *many* are *called* but *few* are *chosen* has a deeper meaning than can be understood at first glance. It indicates that there is something more at work here than just being called and chosen. The principle is one of *individual choice* after being called called , and that choice is to accept Jesus Christ as the Son of God. Every person that has ever lived or will live on earth has been *called* to salvation. To be *chosen* involves a willingness, dedication and faith to perform those things that Christ has chosen us to do. The 12 disciples were chosen by Christ. Every sold-out Christian has active gifts from the Holy Spirit, but many that accept only the calling. The false doctrine of *predestination* is often based upon the misunderstanding of being *chosen*. To accept that God has chosen any individual at birth is just plain contradictory to individual acceptance of Christ by faith. This is borne out in many New Testament scriptures. Salvation is an *individual* choice, and not a predetermined choice made by God. This is, in fact, the fundamental meaning of faith. The fact that from *many* only a *few* will be saved, from all who are saved few will be chosen. The context of chosen in the scripture is a consequence of individual choice, not the will of God. God's choice is for all humanity to be saved; *He would have all men to be saved, and to come to the knowledge of the truth* (I Timothy 2:4). Those who have answered the *call* in faith will be *chosen* (one who is the object of choice or of divine favor: an elect person …Webster).

*So then they which be of faith are blessed with **faithful** Abraham.*   Galatians 3:9

*Fear none of those things which thou shalt suffer: behold, the devil shall cast some of you into prison, that ye may be tried; and ye shall have tribulation ten days: be thou **faithful** unto death, and I will give thee a crown of life.*   Revelation 2:10

This book has been written in an attempt to study the dispensations of time which span the time period between when Adam was created and when there will be a new eternal Kingdom of God. These dispensations, seven in number, have been further linked together by eight different Holy Covenants which were made between man and God. These dispensations and covenants frame the real purpose of this study which is to clearly show that every person who would ever live upon this earth was destined to be saved and enter into an eternal relationship with God and His Son, Jesus Christ. Throughout recorded time, mankind was saved and granted eternal life in the same way; *Believe upon the Lord Jesus Christ and you will be saved.* The entire spectrum of human history has been divided into only two mutually-exclusive periods of time: **before** Christ died for all mankind before the cross of Calvary, and **after** Christ died for all mankind on the cross of Calvary. *Salvation and eternal life* is granted by *grace* to all who believe. How will you spend eternity?

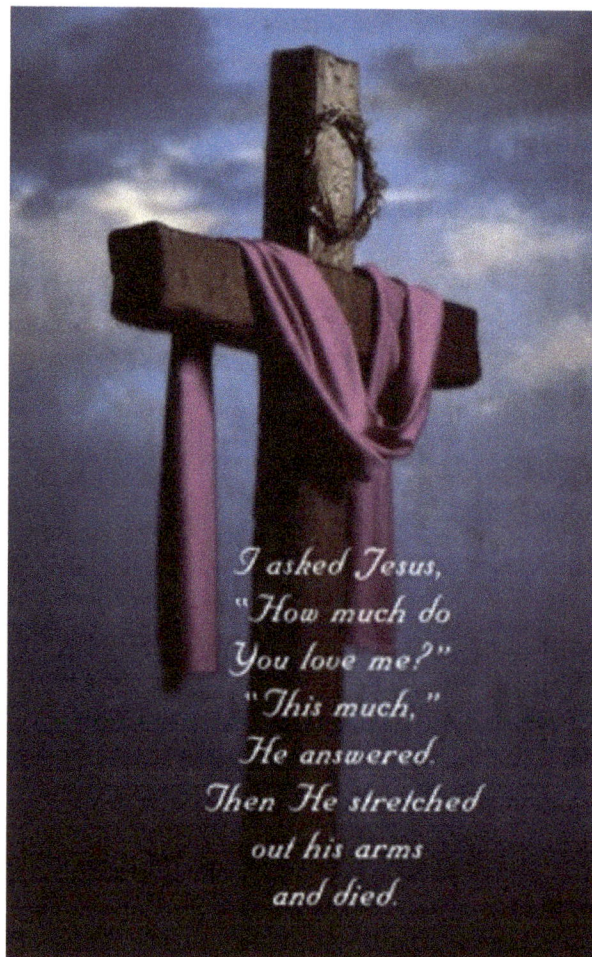

I asked Jesus,
"How much do
You love me?"
"This much,"
He answered.
Then He stretched
out his arms
and died.

BIBLIOGRAPHY

Hall, John J., *God's Dispensational and Prophetic Plan*, John J. Hall, Drawer, J, Newcastle, Oklahoma 73065

Larkin, Clarence, *The Greatest Book on Dispensational Truth in the World*, Clarence Larkin Est., P.O. Box 334, Glenside, Pa. 19038

Thompson A. E., *The New Panorama Bible Study Series*, Fleming H. Revell, Baker Book House, Grand Rapids, Michigan 49516

Ryrie, Charles C., *The Ryrie Study Bible*, Moody Press, Chicago Illinois 1985

Fruchtenbaum, Dr. Arnold G., The Eight Covenants of the Bible, http://www.messianicassociation.org

http://www.gotquestions.org

Other Books by Don T. Phillips

The Book of Revelation: *Mysteries Revealed*

The Book of Exodus: *Historical and Prophetic Truths*

The Birth and Death of Christ

A Biblical Chronology from Adam to Christ

A Sequential Chronology of End Time Events

A Sequential Chronology of End Time Events: *Expanded Edition*

The Book of Ruth: *Historical and Prophetic Truths*

All are available from:

Virtualbookworm Publishing Company, PO Box 9949, College Station Texas, 77842
www.virtualbookworm.com

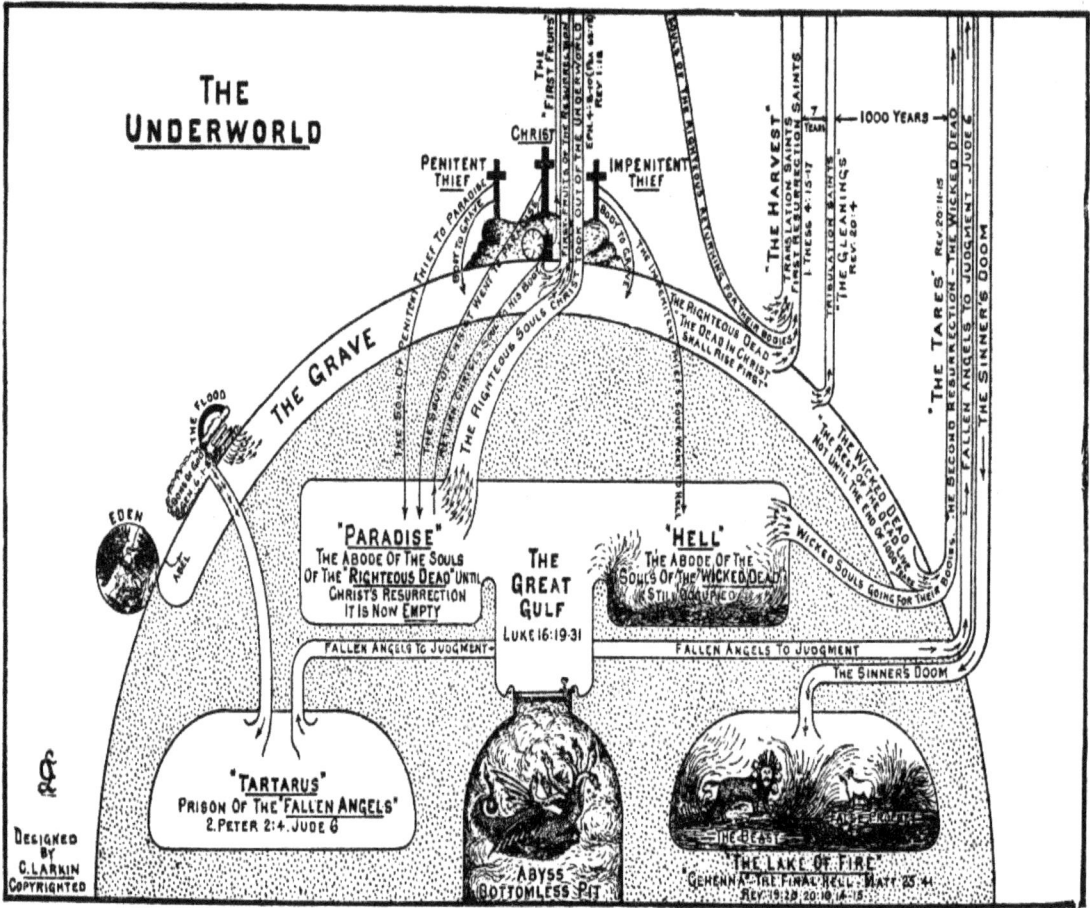

Clarence Larkin (1850-1924)

And, behold, I come quickly; and my reward is with me, to give every man according as his work shall be.

I am Alpha and Omega, the beginning and the end, the first and the last.

Blessed are they that do his commandments, that they may have right to the tree of life, and may enter in through the gates into the city.

Revelation 22: 12-14

www.ingramcontent.com/pod-product-compliance
Lightning Source LLC
Chambersburg PA
CBHW060945100426
42813CB00016B/2871